Borrowed Angel

Borrowed *Angel*

Coping with the Loss of a Child

To the Roos family, I'm so very sorry for your loss. I hope my experiences can bring you a measure of comfort. Thinking of your family,

Erica Kiefer
(Pawranee Shipley's sister)

Erica Kiefer

CURRAWONG PRESS

Currawong Press
110 South 800 West
Brigham City, Utah 84302
http://walnutspringspress.blogspot.com

Text copyright © 2014 by Erica Kiefer
Interior design © 2014 by Currawong Press
Cover design © 2014 by Currawong Press
Illustration *Ty and Jesus* © 2014 by Jean Keaton. Used by permission.

All rights reserved. This book, or parts thereof, may not be reproduced or transmitted in any form, or stored in a database, without prior written permission from the publisher.

ISBN: 978-1-59992-902-6

To my angel Ty:
you are our shining star, guiding us home.

To my husband Dan:
taumafai.

Contents

Acknowledgments 9
Introduction 11
Chapter 1: Searching for Something More 15
Chapter 2: Balancing Motherhood 21
Chapter 3: That Morning 25
Chapter 4: The Life of an Angel 33
Chapter 5: Answers in the Temple 41
Chapter 6: Receiving Comfort 45
Chapter 7: Grieving Differently 53
Chapter 8: Testimony and the Atonement 59
Chapter 9: Battling Guilt 65
Chapter 10: Now and Later 71
Chapter 11: Spiritual Tools 79
Chapter 12: Power in Recreation 87
Chapter 13: Facing Anger 93
Chapter 14: Slowing Down 101
Chapter 15: Tiny Miracles 109
Conclusion: Taumafai 115
Illustration: *Ty and Jesus* 121
About the Author 123

Acknowledgments

Writing on my blog on a weekly (if not daily) basis became a safe haven for my darkest emotions, yet also a way to record uplifting, spiritual experiences that pulled me up from my despair. Writing became so therapeutic because of my family and friends who were willing to hurt and cry with me, and who took the time to send me encouraging messages along the way. To them, I give thanks for suggesting I turn my blog entries into a book.

Gratitude goes to my parents for raising me in the gospel and guiding my testimony. Dad: I appreciate the loving time you spent on this manuscript as my first editor. Khun Maa: thank you for always believing in me and being an example of perseverance. To my siblings and in-laws: The tender ways you honor Ty mean the world to me. Thank you for being a part of his story. To my husband Dan: I would not be as healed without you by my side. I am so lucky to have you in my life!

Thank you for our children, even with their passionate tantrums.

Kalee Crandall and Sann Grave: As my earliest readers, I appreciate the time and emotional energy you spent reviewing my manuscript. Thank you for connecting your loss with mine and for cheering me on throughout the process. Much love to you!

Borrowed Angel would still be trapped in a Word document were it not for my editor, Linda Prince. Linda, I will never forget the moment when I read your email, offering me publication. Thank you for taking a chance on a new author and being an advocate for this book. I admire your ability to add clarity to my writing. Tracy Anderson, I couldn't imagine a more beautiful, perfectly designed cover! Much thanks to my publisher, Walnut Springs Press.

Finally, I express gratitude to my Heavenly Father and Savior Jesus Christ for staying near during my darkest times, and for surrounding me with angels (both in heaven and on earth) to guide me through.

Introduction

I gave up trying to sleep. Every time I closed my eyes, terrifying images from the previous morning flashed through my mind. Instead of dwelling on the sickening fear and disbelief, I opened my laptop and began to write:

> *Twenty-three hours ago, at 8:40 AM, I walked into the nursery to check on my baby, Ty. I didn't see him because he was under his blanket. And when I tore it off, I found him. My baby had died in his sleep.*
>
> *In that moment, despite the sickest of fears in my stomach, I was able to administer CPR to Ty. Dan called the police, and thirty seconds later an officer was inside our home. He took over the CPR, and my hysteria set in.*
>
> *I won't go into the details of the immense fear and panic that took over Dan and me—or the*

unbearable grief when the circle of nurses and doctors stopped using their medical equipment on our son at the hospital. I already wrote that down in a separate, personal account—hoping I could get the images and the sound of our shrieking voices out of my head. But I can't. Every time I close my eyes, that morning replays over and over unmercifully in my mind. And that is not how I want to remember my son. Our son. Our perfect little gift from Heavenly Father that changed our lives and so many others in the short time he was here with us. We know Ty was too good for this world—that his soul is perfect, and that he lives, waiting to reunite with us. He will always be our son, and we will always be a family. Were it not for the truthfulness of this gospel, I could not bear it.

At the hospital, we were allowed to hold our son for the next hour and a half. He looked so beautiful and peaceful, even in death. He was wrapped in a white blanket, and as I held his body against my chest, I kissed the tiny bridge between his eyes—just like I always did before putting him to sleep. Sleep, my little angel.

I know Ty will be watching over us and waiting for his mother and father to live righteous lives on this earth and be with him again. He is our motivator, because we know we will be with him again after this mortal life if we live good lives.

Thank you for your thoughts and prayers. Yesterday was the hardest day of our lives. And we hope today will be the second-hardest day, and tomorrow the third—that it will get easier with each passing day. Since yesterday morning, I can feel the Spirit wrapping around us and comforting us. And in those moments, I am calm and feel so at peace, knowing Ty was welcomed home by his grandpa Kiefer, who was able to send him on his way to earth, and receive him back with open arms. Ty was not alone. He was not afraid.

My mortal, physical self can't help but give in to the grief and anguish that is ours to bear. And it's okay to hurt. To be confused and broken inside. As long as Heavenly Father continues to persevere with His comforting Spirit, we will be okay.

It's going to hurt for a long, long time. No parents should have to go through this—no matter how old their child is. But we will heal. I have faith in that. Dan and I have the most amazing family and friends, who literally swarmed around us all day and night, even if it took planes or cars to get here.

We love you and thank you,

Erica and Dan

With this letter, I announced to our family and friends that our four-and-a-half-month-old son, our only child, had passed away. However, just as important, I shared a piece of my testimony—a testimony that would grow substantially as my husband and I traveled through the gauntlet of grief, escaping miraculously with healing wounds.

This book incorporates the details of our journey, reflecting on our heartbreak as parents, but also our spiritual growth as a son and daughter of a loving Heavenly Father who would not let us suffer alone.

I hope the story of my borrowed angel will help you cope with your loss, or help you understand the grief of someone who has experienced a tragic loss of their own.

Chapter 1

Searching for Something More

For four and a half years I embraced rugby as a colossal piece of my identity. When I played, I felt confident and accomplished. In fact, nothing was more exhilarating or fulfilling than sprinting down the field, gripping the ball in my hands and sidestepping my opponents to score. I remember crying to my husband that I knew I wanted kids someday—I've always known that—but I feared I would never feel as good about myself as I did on the rugby field. Dan soothed my concerns, promising I'd feel joy as a mother. I could only try my best to believe that would be true.

Months after we graduated from college, my husband and I decided to expand our family. A sudden longing and readiness for a baby struck with such force that I was not prepared for the period of rejection, stress, and anxiety that followed. Despite a series of doctor appointments and fertility medication, my body—which seemed to shut down within a couple months of trying to conceive—was still not cooperating.

Some people might judge me, saying that just over a year is not long, even for people without fertility problems. That may be so; however, the challenge for me didn't lie in waiting. If I had been told I needed to wait a certain amount of time before conception happened, perhaps I would have handled it better. Given a timeline, wouldn't we all accept challenges with a readier heart? But for years I have struggled with fear of the unknown and jumping to the worst conclusions. What if I could never have children and this was only the beginning of a long road of failure? Fear inhibited my patience and my faith.

After thirteen months of frustration and dismay, I finally presented the problem to the Lord with the truest of intentions. I felt impressed to attend the temple—and not just attend but to go alone for my first time. Before I left, I knelt by my bed and offered a tearful, heartfelt prayer to our Father in Heaven, emphasizing my desire for comfort, knowledge, and most importantly, hope.

After almost bailing out on my plan because of the cold December weather and misplacing my recommend, I sleepily completed an endowment session before entering the celestial room. The peace in the celestial room brought me fully awake, reminding me of my intended purpose for coming to the temple. I sat quietly, unsure what to expect, and pondered the promise in my patriarchal blessing that guidance would be given to me in the temple. After a few minutes of struggling to focus next to a chatty pair of friends, I opened my eyes in slight annoyance and caught sight of a Bible. The thought crossed my mind to flip through it.

Skeptical of whether the thought was a prompting or just me talking to myself, I grabbed the white Bible and moved to a secluded chair. I turned the pages with no idea what I was looking for. My attention fell on the book of Samuel in the Old Testament. I read the first chapter a couple times through, as I was unfamiliar with the story. But I felt connected to the woman named Hannah. In her sorrows, she wept and prayed to the Lord to bless her with a son because "the Lord had shut up her womb"[1] and she "was in bitterness of soul."[2] When the Lord remembered her and she conceived a son, Hannah named him Samuel, a Hebrew name that means "requested of the Lord."

Feeling inspired by the strength and prayerful nature of this woman, whose feelings and desire tread so close to my heart, I couldn't help but feel connected to verse 27, which says, "For this child I prayed; and the Lord hath given me my petition which I asked of him."[3] I read that verse over and over again, waiting for an overwhelming feeling of confirmation that the Lord was answering my prayer. But uncertainty made me question the experience.

Not until I was driving home in the car and sharing the experience with Dan over the phone did a happy spirit clear my doubts. My husband asked me, "Do you really think that after praying to the Lord for an answer, you just happened to open to that story?" Reassured by Dan's words and the renewed feeling in my heart, I held onto the hope that our future would surely include a child. The Lord had answered my prayer.

The following day at church, my husband and I met with the bishop for tithing settlement. While we spoke with him and mentioned our efforts to conceive, I saw tears in his eyes. He expressed his feelings that "good things" were coming our way in 2009. As he gave Dan a blessing of comfort, the bishop stated that Dan was a good husband and would enjoy the blessings of fatherhood in the upcoming year. The bishop also declared that we would be "blessed with all our righteous desires." Surprised by the boldness of this promise, coupled with my experience in the temple, Dan and I entered 2009 with bolstered faith and assurance.

Two months later, after a seemingly endless number of negative pregnancy tests, I found myself staring with disbelief at the positive test in my hand. I checked and rechecked the instructions, analyzing the results until I convinced myself there was no possible way I was reading it wrong. Really, truly, I was pregnant!

People often asked me if it was the final refill of Clomid that helped produced this wonderful event. I would reply that I'm sure it helped. But in my mind, I remembered the promise I received in the temple and offered silent thanks to a loving Heavenly Father.

The glowing, radiating energy that comes with pregnancy followed me through the whole course of carrying my son—minus a mere month and a half of mild sickness. My blissful pregnancy seemed uncannily comfortable and easy. As my husband described me,

"You are the most unhormonal woman I have ever met." It was his way of complimenting me, while expressing gratitude that he had dodged the emotional chaos that might have otherwise transpired.

Still, as the final months approached, I couldn't shake the biting anxiety that something might happen to my baby. As I watched other pregnant women grow, I questioned my comparatively small belly. True, I carried well and exercised throughout my pregnancy. Even so, the worry over my son's safety amplified two weeks before his due date. I noticed he moved less, and while testing seemed to prove otherwise, I was sure I was leaking amniotic fluid.

Five days prior to my due date, I still felt compelled to check on my son's condition. I met with a perinatologist who performed a non-stress test on my baby. Ty's heart rate checked out just fine. However, twice they measured my amniotic fluid levels. The perinatologist indicated, with some concern in her voice, that she could barely find any fluid inside me—which in part explained my smaller belly, but most importantly, the lack of movement from my baby.

While Ty seemed to be fairing well enough at the moment, the doctor explained that the baby could sit on his cord or lack sufficient cushioning and I wouldn't know it until it was too late. "So," she continued, "I think we need to send you to Labor and Delivery to be induced."

My eyes filled with tears—a combination of excitement and trepidation—as I managed to say to my mother beside me, "I'm having my baby today!"

Labor was a whirlwind of surprise, fearful intensity, and pure joy. With Cervidil inserted to soften my cervix at 4:00 PM, the supposed plan included sleeping at the hospital, followed by induction with Pitocin at 5:00 the next morning. However, at a staggering pace, Ty Edward Kiefer made his entrance into this world that night at 11:26, weighing six pounds eleven ounces and measuring nineteen and a half inches long. His arrival came so quickly that I survived a natural birth without even having a chance to receive an epidural. Never in my life have I felt more proud.

Still shaking in recovery, I held my infant son in my arms, in awe of the adoration I felt for him, and the instant bond between mother and child. With my husband at my side, we cherished our newest family member, unable to imagine a happy life without him.

Naive and inexperienced, I once thought life as a rugby player was as a good as it gets—that I might never feel as satisfied or confident with my accomplishments. How I laugh at myself now, recalling the unparalleled experience of birthing a child and being a mother. Having tasted the fruit, I never wanted anything more.

Notes

1. 1 Samuel 1:5.
2. Ibid, v. 10.
3. Ibid., v. 27.

Chapter 2

Balancing Motherhood

My mother was right. While I was pregnant, she told me I would finally know how much she loves me. In the weeks following Ty's birth, I wrote her a letter expressing that now I understood what she meant. As I cradled a piece of heaven on my chest, my heart nearly burst, straining against the magnitude of love that grew each day.

I remember commenting to my friend long before Ty was born, "Sometimes I wish I could skip the baby stage and jump right into the cute toddler stage!" I can still see the way she knowingly shook her head at me, eyeing her three young children at her feet, and said it would be different when it was my own baby. Like my mother, she was right.

As I held my tiny, angelic newborn, his pure spirit seemed to linger a baby-sized hand away from heaven. I realize now why people are so drawn to newborns. It is because their perfect spirits remind us of the home we once came from, and of an eternal plan so much greater than we fully comprehend. I believe a quiet part of our spirit has the capacity to be touched by that of a newborn, gently awakening things we once knew but have forgotten because of the veil.

As a new mother, I began to understand the meaning of sacrifice as I underwent the interrupted nights of sleep, arranged my life around pumping and feedings, as well as diaper changing, and developed mastitis, an excruciatingly painful condition, within two weeks of Ty's birth. But I just couldn't complain too much. I kept reminding myself how desperately I wanted him and how grateful I was to have a healthy, beautiful boy home with me at last. My patience as a mother surpassed anything I might have credited myself with. I realized that my struggle and fear of not conceiving had fortified my patience, and most importantly, increased the value I placed in motherhood.

Most days and nights, I learned to laugh through the difficult times. Finding reasons to smile at my little guy was not difficult, though. During the day, he lay calm and mellow, and so serious with his peaceful demeanor. At night, he only fussed when he needed a diaper change or a quick feeding and then went right back to sleep—except for the one time I was in the middle of changing his diaper and he started screaming. With the dim nightlight, I couldn't figure out why he was uncharacteristically upset—until I felt the warm liquid all over his eyes and face. He had shot himself in the face with his own urine. Oh, that driving instinct to care for our young when they are in pain or in need!

I still smile when I reminisce over my first date-night with my husband. We had enjoyed parenthood for one month and were celebrating by eating dinner at our favorite restaurant. After we ordered a meal to share, minutes passed before I commented on our body language: both of us had an elbow on the table, resting a heavy head in one hand and looking off in the distance without even speaking to each other. The passing waiters probably thought we were the most unromantic, boring couple they'd ever served. Laughing after I pointed this out, we half jokingly considered skipping the movie to spend our date-night napping.

Despite sleep deprivation, Dan and I greeted each of Ty's milestones with sheer delight—the first bath; that invigorating four-hour stretch of sleep; the tiny smile that surely wasn't gas this time; rolling over; that incredible, heart-melting laughter; the first night sleeping in the crib; the first bite of "solid" food . . .

However, there were times when I struggled to balance my life as a mother and wife, with two part-time jobs, exercise, and other hobbies and activities on my list. Less than two months into this, I was still figuring out how to do it all, without making time for naps.

One day, my morning began differently. I didn't rush to arise and pack up the baby and everything else I would need for the day. I didn't hurry to my dad's house to exercise, followed by jetting out the door to complete my to-do list.

Instead, I woke up a little later than intended just before my visiting teachers arrived. They offered a lesson on compassionate service and brought a wonderful spirit into my home. It was a peace that had been lacking, especially over the past two weeks. In our discussion, I found myself sharing with these two women how we all need to have quiet moments in our day in order to feel the Spirit and allow promptings to find their way into our hearts. When my friends left, with my own words ringing in my ears, I realized a few things. First, I needed to slow down. I was exhausting myself when there were other solutions. I needed to reprioritize my priorities. In my whirlwind days, I allowed life to distract me from simply holding my boy and snuggling him. My sudden insight was not so much an epiphany as a willingness to accept the needed changes in my life, so that I would never take my son for granted.

I cradled Ty in the rocking chair that morning, ignoring the reminders of things I really *could* be doing. Instead, I savored the pleasure of kissing my baby's sweet face and feeling his little hands clinging to my chest. My to-do list that day became simple: love my son and enjoy my time with him as his mother.

Months later, I would be ever grateful for the whispered teachings of the Spirit that allowed me to grow as a mother and enjoy that precious moment (and countless others) with my son. Had I known how limited my time with him would be, I might never have let him go.

Chapter 3

That Morning

On March 10, 2010, Dan and I talked together while we lay in bed for just a few minutes longer. The nursery across the hall remained quiet, but I didn't wait much longer before checking on Ty.

I walked into the nursery and peered into the crib. It looked empty, except for the baby quilt crumpled in the middle. Confused, and knowing he must be under there, I held my breath, fear tightening my chest. I tore off the blanket and saw Ty lying there, motionless. In horror, I shrieked Dan's name as I scooped up our son's limp body.

Even from the bedroom, Dan seemed to know. He yelled, "No! No!" over and over, running into the nursery as I lay Ty on the changing table. Dan's hollering continued, his voice weighted with terror and anger.

"Stop it! Dan, stop it!" Though my heart still pounded, a sudden calmness came over me, and I could think with clarity. I asked Dan to call the police, which seemed to bring him out of his shock. "Okay," he said, grabbing his phone.

While he spoke with dispatch, I placed my mouth over Ty's and gave him two breaths, but they didn't seem to work. I swiped his tiny mouth with one finger and then pushed against his tongue. I attempted the breaths again, and relief swept through me as I watched Ty's chest rise and fall. Having received my CPR certification practicing on adult mannequins, I never thought my first time performing CPR would be on my four-and-a-half-month-old son. But there I was, adjusting his forehead and chin to an angle where I could gently breathe air into him. I pumped his chest with two fingers, watching a hint of blue fade from his lips.

Much of the anxiety left my body. I thought I would save him. This is why I had been trained in CPR for the last five years, my job aside. I would save my son.

My efforts lasted less than a minute before Dan let a police officer into our home. I stepped aside and allowed him to take over. Dan and I watched him examine Ty as we struggled to fight off the consuming fear. The paramedics arrived a couple minutes later and set up equipment in the living room. Trained help had arrived, and I thought—dared to hope—everything might be okay. However, when the officer fled from the nursery with my son in his arms, my hysteria set in. It was in that moment that I realized I was no longer in control. My son's life was literally out of my hands, and there was nothing more I could do.

Screaming "Please save my baby," I chased after the officer, who handed Ty to the paramedics. Dan grabbed me and pulled me into his chest, preventing me from witnessing the scene. We clung to each other, both crying and praying out loud, begging God not to take our son. I told Heavenly Father I would be the best mother if He'd only save Ty and give me this one more chance. My soul was filled with desperation and terror. Stepping away from me, Dan punched holes in the nursery wall, each one an evidence of his agony.

An investigator and policewoman kept us in the nursery. Regaining temporary composure, Dan held me in the rocking chair while we waited to hear our baby cry again. But the only sound was our own grief. As parents we felt powerless. We could do nothing but pray and console one another, quieting each other's fears before unleashing our wild terror all over again.

Just as the paramedics drove away with Ty in the ambulance, my dad arrived to take Dan and me to the hospital. After collapsing and sobbing in my dad's arms, I couldn't think of what I needed. I had no idea what I was supposed to do. Shock had set in. The female police officer verbally guided me step by step to find a bra, to find my socks, my shoes, and my wallet. Like a zombie, I followed her instructions before leaving home.

Concerned neighbors watched from a distance. In my hazy state, the gravity of the situation struck me again, and I fell apart in the car. As we drove to the hospital, I knew things would never be the same. Even if Ty were to live, with the lack of oxygen to his brain he would not be the same little boy we put to bed last night. We tried to figure out the timeline of his last breaths. I had checked on him at 4:00 AM. Dan checked on him at 7:00. We didn't make it into the nursery again until 8:40.

In the emergency room, it sickened me to see Ty's little body on the table, surrounded by doctors and nurses and medical tools that seemed too large and much too severe for him. Still, Dan and I had to keep hoping. As long as they worked on our baby, there was still hope.

The moment felt surreal—madness whirling around Dan and me as we gripped each other's hands. This couldn't be happening, not to us. Not after everything we'd learned and been through while waiting for Ty's birth. Not after God promised him to me.

When the doctor approached us with remorse in his eyes, admitting there was nothing more they could do for our son, Dan and I crumpled to the floor, wailing in each other's arms.

"That's my baby! My boy!"

In the movies, it almost seems a stereotypical reaction to hear the mother crying "No! No! No, no, no!" over and over, as if that would change anything—as if she could trade in her broken heart to alter the outcome. But there I was, playing the role of the shattered mother, crippled beside her agonized husband, suffering the same excruciating pain.

It was only a few minutes before a nurse wrapped Ty in a white knitted blanket and let me hold him. His body felt so empty. But I cradled him close to my chest and he still felt like my baby. I kissed the small bridge between his eyes as I always did before naps and bedtime. Ty appeared so peaceful and beautiful, like he was sleeping—a little angel in my arms. I rocked him and loved him with Dan crying beside me and holding Ty's chubby hand.

"Taumafai," I murmured, and Dan began to sing the Samoan hymn "Taumafai"—a song that speaks of persevering when the road becomes tough, of relying on Christ and hoping for the future. If we rely on Him, the lyrics say, we can do all things. "Taumafai" was Dan's favorite song on his mission in New Zealand, and he'd sung it there on days when he needed extra strength. During our five years of marriage, he had sung the song to me from time to time when nothing else could console me. It had always brought us peace in the past, as it did that day in the hospital while we embraced our son.

A peaceful spirit entered the room, reminding us that Ty was with his grandpa Kiefer, who passed away a year and half before, and with Jesus Christ and Heavenly Father. A blanket of strength wrapped around us, confirming in our hearts that Ty was safe and happy, but worried about our grief for him.

We held our baby's body for the next hour, savoring the warmth of his skin before it faded away. Dan and I (and even Ty) received blessings of comfort from my father and one of Dan's good friends. When it was time to let Ty go, Dan and I each held him one more time, unwilling to believe this would be the last time we would carry him in our arms. The ER doctor wanted to speak with us, and we finally left our little Bubs behind so a kind bereavement specialist could make molds of his hands and feet.

Speaking with the doctor, we were touched by the sorrow in his eyes. Our son's death was not simply a part of his job. The experience of trying to save Ty's life was personal and painful, and the doctor felt deeply for us. He explained that as far as they could tell, our son had passed away from sudden infant death syndrome (SIDS). He told us what we already knew—that little was known about what causes SIDS.

Harrowed with guilt, I dared to ask the question tearing me apart inside. "Was it because the blanket was over him?" I winced, remembering how I couldn't see Ty—how he was completely covered by it.

The doctor reassured me that a baby blanket is much too lightweight to suffocate an infant of Ty's size and ability, despite the precautions given to new parents. Dan also reminded me that Ty was a strong boy who could lift his head and roll over both ways. The doctor explained that there seems to be a biological and chemical problem in the brain of SIDS babies that impedes their respiratory system. I felt some momentary relief by this news, as did my husband, but the guilt would still plague us in future days.

Dan and I returned to my dad's condo—a home we had lived in during the first four years of marriage. It felt safe. It felt like the only place we could go. We never wanted to step foot into our own apartment again.

Dan and I walked around the neighborhood before we entered the condo. Hand in hand we tried to comprehend how our lives had changed in what seemed an instant. More importantly, we discussed what we were going to do about it. Dan held me in front of him and asked me, with urgency in his voice, to make a promise with him—that we would always be there for each other and rely on one another, that we would include God in our struggle to heal and never turn our backs on Him.

Through our embrace, we began the crucial first step of our grief. We reinforced a solid union between husband and wife and God, securing a foundation that would bring us closer, despite the precious life we once knew lying in ruins before us.

A day at a time, a week at a time, we hoped and prayed we would survive this.

Chapter 4

The Life of an Angel

During the three days leading up to the funeral, our friends and immediate family members flooded the condo. My brothers and their wives drove from Salt Lake City to Provo each day, while other family members and friends traveled from Arizona, Nevada, North Carolina, and New Jersey. My mother came all the way from Thailand.

Dan and I cried off and on with every first hug, feeling the depth of mourning from our loved ones. Friends and neighbors showered us with meals, flowers, sympathy cards, books, and generous donations of money. Astounded by this compassion and service, Dan and I wept with gratitude.

On the night of Ty's passing, Dan and I couldn't fall asleep, though we were exhausted. Every time we closed our eyes, horrific memories attacked us. Late in the night, when I wasn't cringing and whimpering from the nightmares, I managed to doze off. At Dan's request, a couple friends and family members spent the night with us in the living room, sprawled out on the floor and the leather sectional. Dan felt safer when the condo was full of people, with a movie droning in the background. Even still, by the time the morning light crept through the windows, he had not slept at all. He would be fearful of the quiet, lonely darkness for months to come.

Reflecting on Ty's life is what brought us peace in the days leading up to the funeral. The night before our baby passed away, Dan and I each had a special moment with him. Knowing Ty had taught us well would calm our hearts in the days to come.

At the beginning of March, just over a week before Ty passed away, life started to become busy again. I had agreed to pick up an extra twelve hours of work as a substitute recreation therapist for the next two months. This required me to leave Ty with his grandpa Rock for about three hours in the afternoon, Tuesday through Friday. On the night before Ty passed away, I was running a little late after work. I hurried into the condo, so excited to see my boy. I felt anxious being away from him, and felt worse when my dad commented, "I think he missed you today." Ty wasn't crying, but we both lit up at the sight of each other.

With Dan exercising downstairs, and my dad still home, I could have left Ty with them and rushed to my church meeting after dinner, but something gave me cause for hesitation. Sensing the importance of spending time with him, I drove Ty back to our apartment and nursed him, rather than offer him the prepared bottle.

I will never forget the beautiful way Ty gazed up at me, as he often did when he nursed. His calm demeanor added to the loving expression on his face, his eyes deep and serious. My heart soared with love for him, and I didn't care that I would be thirty minutes late to my meeting. That moment was all about my son and me, sharing the bond of motherhood. I remembered the prompting I had received a couple months previously to slow down my life and not take my son for granted. That night, Ty again reminded me to cherish these quiet moments with my child, when the Spirit could speak to us and help me be the mother I wanted to be.

By the time I returned home from my meeting, it was after nine PM. Just as I started wondering why the apartment was so quiet and dim, Dan surprised me by hurrying over from the nursery with the proudest smile on his face. He couldn't wait to tell me about the wonderful evening he'd shared with Ty. Even though the baby was fussy and crying after I left, Dan said he put his law books aside and didn't worry about studying. His patience held, even when his efforts to console Ty took extra time and effort. In the past, Dan might have become frustrated when he was unable to comfort our son in the same way I could. But that night, Dan said he simply laughed at Ty's sleepy efforts to stay awake, until he finally fell asleep on Dan's shoulder. Reluctant to put Ty down, Dan held him for fifteen more minutes, savoring the experience.

Peering into the crib, Dan and I beamed at our cute boy, who stirred awake with a restlessness that was more distressed than usual. He seemed to be fighting sleep, but his exhaustion was clearly winning. With so much love flooding the nursery, I wanted to pick him and just hold him some more, but I didn't want to ruin Dan's satisfaction of putting him to bed.

I smiled at how proud my husband felt as a dad—that tonight, he had conquered his impatience. Dan will always remember this final night as the pivotal moment when Ty taught him to truly be a father. After his passing, Dan and I often spoke of the perfect night each of us had with Ty, and the uncanny way in which the Lord seemed to have prepared us for our baby's death. It began during my pregnancy when I kept feeling I might lose him, and continued after his birth. Some of that worry was a natural part of parenthood, but in the weeks leading up to Ty's death, our concern about SIDS amplified. We were extra worried because Ty started sleeping so well on his tummy that even when we turned him onto his back, he would roll right back over. My dad also seemed unable to shake the worry, despite having raised his children during the generation of "tummy sleeping" with little concern. When he babysat, my dad found himself frequently checking on Ty during naps, as though something might happen to him. The behavior was highly uncharacteristic of my dad's rational personality. These feelings led Dan to give Ty a blessing of safety more than once, including two nights before he passed away. That day was his four-month checkup, where the pediatrician deemed Ty perfectly healthy. Upon my mentioning the baby's natural inclination to sleep on his stomach, the physician's assistant warned me about the higher correlation with SIDS, and how one death happens every year to a family in the community. I never believed that family would be mine.

Still, his advice frightened Dan and me. On the last night after putting Ty to bed, Dan and I sat in our room continuing the discussion. I asked, "What happens if I go check on Ty and he is not breathing?" Dan told me to give him CPR, something I had felt I needed to know since Ty was born. Fortunately, because of the types of jobs I'd had for the past five years, I'd been trained in CPR annually. Still, I asked for clarification on a baby. The disturbing conversation led us back into the nursery to roll Ty onto his back. He flipped right back over onto his tummy. There was nothing we could do.

After the incident the next morning, I often wondered what the point was in somehow anticipating Ty's death—having SIDS on our minds, even to point of discussing the CPR that I would perform on my son, when it still didn't save him in the end. Dan and I came to the conclusion that the purpose of my knowledge and calm ability to perform CPR in that crucial moment was to eliminate regret. We did all we could with no precious time wasted—even the miracle of the police officer arriving at our home within thirty seconds of the 911 call. We heard later that he had been in the middle of a routine traffic stop just outside our neighborhood.

One final element that allows us to believe Ty's passing was according to God's plan was finding out that two members from my dad's ward had put his name on the temple prayer roll. The night before Ty died, one woman suggested to her friend that she didn't know why, but she felt Jeff Rock's name should be added to the prayer roll, even though she did not know him very well. We believe this extra blessing is what allowed my dad to maintain his composure when he received the call from the police to take us to the hospital. The police officer admitted that routine protocol discourages calling family members to a crisis scene because of the added emotional stress and panic. However, when he heard my dad lived down the street, the police officer had no qualms about calling him to assist us. Stoic in his strength, my dad comforted us, despite his own anguish.

Looking back, we see how the Lord prepared us to treasure every moment with Ty. I've often wondered if the four and a half months was a gift in itself—that perhaps Ty, with his perfect spirit only needing a body, might have passed sooner, but the Lord in His mercy allowed us the memories, as well as the time needed for Ty to teach us about parenthood, paving the way for future siblings.

My mother was one of many people who felt a special connection to Ty. Perhaps it was because she'd stepped into my hospital room just in time to witness his speedy arrival into this world, or maybe the fact that her prolonged visit from Thailand had allowed her to bond with him during the first five weeks of his life. Whatever the reason, Ty's death had an impact on my mother's life in ways we never expected.

After suffering hardships throughout her life, my mother was inactive in the Church for a number of years, though I believe her testimony of the gospel remained intact. A month after Ty's death, while my mother was visiting from Thailand again, she went to Relief Society with me. During the small portion of time allotted for the sharing of testimonies, she unexpectedly stood up and announced with resolution that she was "back." She committed to do whatever it took to be with her sweet grandson again for the eternities. We embraced and shed tears together, and my mother continues to work toward the promise that "families can be together forever."

Held on Saturday, March 13, Ty's funeral proved to be the most beautiful experience of my life. The heavens wept with us on that cold, rainy day, with not an ounce of sunshine touching the ashen sky. As Dan and I entered our church building, the Brigham Young University men's rugby team greeted us unexpectedly, filling the foyer. Wearing their athletic warm-ups, Dan's former teammates and coaches sang to us, their voices touching our hearts with the LDS hymn "Ye Elders of Israel," and the Primary song "Army of Helaman." Sobbing, Dan and I held each other, overcome by the love and support emanating from these men. As the rugby players and coaches exited the church, each of them embraced Dan and me. And while they could not attend the funeral, they told us they would be dedicating their game that day to our son, Ty Edward Kiefer.

Strengthened and better prepared, Dan and I went into the viewing room. An overwhelming spirit of peace and comfort eventually calmed our weeping. Everything about the room was perfect, especially the abundance of flowers dressing the room in soft blue, white, and yellow. Wanting flowers more than anything to contribute to honoring Ty, Dan and I could not have been more pleased. No one could deny the Spirit that permeated the glowing room. Our baby boy looked beautiful, evidence of the delicate manner in which he was dressed in white by the tender hands of women in our family.

From what I was told, the service itself was "the single most spiritual event" some people had ever attended. Many would say they had never seen a funeral as exquisite and elegant as they witnessed that day. Over three hundred people attended the service, and I'm sure all would agree that the Spirit in the chapel seemed almost tangible, as though the crowded room was fuller still with spirits and angels, honoring a perfect soul who had returned to heaven.

As he is for my mother, Ty is our motivation—our reminder to work hard to accomplish things that truly matter in this life. He is our guardian angel guiding us home.

Chapter 5

Answers in the Temple

Having been physically stripped of motherhood, I hungered for a baby. Within days of Ty's passing, I feared some people might judge me as callous for even thinking about another baby so soon, but having lost a colossal part of my identity—a core piece of my life—I seemed unable to stifle my soul's yearning.

Never in my life have I felt such loss and desperation. Nine months seemed an eternity to wait, let alone the time it might take to conceive. Guilt struck me every time I had to dump my breast milk as I transitioned from a nursing mother. Sobbing through the process, I felt as if I was betraying my body. I was supposed to be nurturing a baby, and my body knew that just as much as my emotions. The chasm of grief compelled me to pray again for comfort regarding children.

Ten days after Ty passed away, Dan and I sought refuge in the temple. Acting as proxies for deceased individuals, we wept over the altar in the sealing room. The promises of eternal families never meant more to us than it did that day, as we remembered with gratitude the blessings of being sealed in the temple for all time and eternity. We would be with our son again.

Upon request, Dan and I were permitted to enter the celestial room. In that very room over one year previously, I had received personal revelation that I would be granted a child. Now, sitting on a couch with Dan beside me, I flipped again to 1 Samuel and read the chapter about Hannah. I reflected on the conversation I had with my sister-in-law Carrie on the evening after the funeral.

In comparing my life with the story of Hannah, I commented that I always thought Ty would be immune from this kind of tragedy, despite my frequent worrying about him. He had been promised to me, and while I did not feel angry at the Lord, I did not fully understand why He would take my son back so soon. Carrie reminded me of the rest of the story—that Hannah vowed to give Samuel back to the Lord if He would grant her a son. "Therefore also I have lent him to the Lord; as long as he liveth he shall be lent to the Lord. And he worshipped the Lord there."[1]

Dumbfounded, I realized I had never considered that part of the story to be applicable. Surely, Ty is performing important work for our Heavenly Father, just as Samuel ministered on earth from a young age. The Lord blessed me with Ty long enough for him to gain the body he needed to be a part of this eternal plan, and then he returned to continue the Lord's work.

As I sat in the celestial room, once again pondering that chapter, as well as the future of my family, the thought came to me, "Read on." I read the entire second chapter of 1 Samuel, as well as skimming through other portions of the Bible. However, only a small part of 1 Samuel 2 lingered in my memory by the time I exited the temple. Those particular verses speak of Samuel ministering before the Lord, just as Hannah promised he would. Subsequently, because Hannah lent her son to Lord, He blessed her with three more sons and two daughters. In a sense, the Lord paid Hannah back five-fold for her sacrifice.[2] What I once considered a sad story of a barren woman who gives up her only son to the Lord, in fact has a happier, merciful ending.

When I shared my thoughts with Dan, he beamed all day. He too seemed to feel the promise that more children would come into our family. It was another confirmation to me that the Lord had not forgotten us. There was hope in our future once again.

These experiences would not be the last time attending the temple brought me comfort. Four months after Ty passed away, my brother Ryan, his wife Emily, and their daughter Adelyn were sealed for time and all eternity. As Ryan and Emily knelt across from each other at the altar, family and friends in attendance wiped tears from their eyes. Having witnessed the beginning of Ryan and Emily's journey, we knew their story would now never end—that they would forever be connected as family.

Following Ryan and Emily's sealing, a temple worker brought four-month-old Addie into the room, wearing a beautiful white dress. Emily's mom carried the baby to the altar. When Addie's little hand was placed on top of Ryan and Emily's, it seemed everyone started to cry. I couldn't tell for sure because of the tears blurring my vision. The Spirit was there in abundance, surrounding that family and touching all of us.

I will always remember the image of Ryan, Emily, and Addie gathered around the altar. I will also never forget how Addie, with her unusually calm demeanor, stared at me the entire time. Seated in the front row, I was not directly across from her, but her eyes found mine and did not leave my gaze. She did not even blink—just watched me with a look I pondered over for days. She seemed so attentive and aware, and I have no doubt she was seeing things with her pure spirit that the rest of us could not see.

Then she smiled at me, an expression forever imprinted in my memory. She was a visual reminder for Dan and me of the same blessings we share because Ty was born in the covenant. Just as Addie's hand touched her parents' in a symbol of their eternal sealing as a family, Dan and I feel Ty's hand on ours. Our bond will last for eternity if we keep the promises we have made. I treasure that day in the temple.

Notes

1. 1 Samuel 1:28.
2. See 1 Samuel 2:18–21.

Chapter 6

Receiving Comfort

While the first two weeks following Ty's death were the most shocking and heartbreaking, I also felt closer to Heavenly Father and the spirit world than I ever had in my life. In the days leading up to the funeral, I questioned why I was not locked up in my bedroom crying all day and all night. Not that the tears weren't flowing regularly, because they certainly were, but there was a sizable amount of peace I never would have imagined I could feel so soon.

Two nights before the funeral, my husband offered me an answer that I immediately felt to be true. With his voice quivering with emotion and love, Dan said, "As soon as Ty passed away, his spirit rallied up all the angels and spirits in heaven and told them to please go be with his mother—that because a mother's love for her child far surpasses anything else in this world, she would need all the comfort she could receive, because if she were to feel the pain in its entirety, she could not bear it."

Dan and I truly felt enveloped by an unseen army of angels. My experience in those early days testified to me that during our hardest times, the Lord does not leave us alone. He surrounds us with angels and spirits of loved ones who have passed before us, whose job it is to bolster us with strength. In addition, with so many prayers by friends and family all around the world, we truly felt the power of prayer. The Lord does not ignore His children's pleadings to comfort their loved ones. I also learned that in order to feel this comfort, I must be receptive to it. This required effort through constant prayer, as well as reading the scriptures and the words of the living prophets so I could be in a mental and spiritual place to recognize the Lord's comfort.

When I was young, the plan of salvation was my favorite topic in Primary. I was in such awe of the fact that we were spirit daughters and sons of Heavenly Father before we came to this earth and that we would live and be tested in mortality, and then die and return to be with Him, as well as all our friends and family. I thought it was such a wonderful idea. At the age of nine, I remember helping my younger sister with her Primary talk and excitedly making a poster featuring a simple diagram of the plan of salvation. Even back then, I felt I understood it so well, and with the trust and confidence of a child, I never questioned the truthfulness of it. Little did I know how desperately I would cling to this gospel principle some twenty years later.

After Ty's funeral, I stopped by the cemetery almost on a daily basis. How could I not, when it was a mere half mile up the road and one of the most beautifully groomed places in Provo? How could I not, when my son lay just beyond my reach? I sat beside Ty's grave, reflecting on this new life of mine: "Did this really happen to me? Is this really my life?" When the answer was inevitably yes, I'd sit and pray for comfort and imagine what my son was doing at that very moment. He was indeed *somewhere* and just as alive as when I held him in my arms. I just couldn't see him anymore.

One afternoon, I sat with amplified understanding beside Ty's grave. For an instant, I seemed to fully grasp the words the Lord spoke to Joseph Smith as he suffered in Liberty Jail: "Thine adversity and thine afflictions shall be but a small moment."[1] I truly felt that my separation from Ty would not be for long—that our reunion was not far away. Through the plan of salvation, I would be with him again. This assurance brought so much peace to my heart that I smiled with relief on that sunny day. I held onto an anxious excitement for the Millennium to come, sensing it was just around the corner. I would hold my resurrected son and be able to raise him from infancy through adulthood in a better world. It was not far away at all.

Since then I have realized my feelings did not necessarily mean the Millennium would come in only a few years, or even in my lifetime. What I was feeling on that day in the cemetery was the Lord's perspective of time and eternity—that what we perceive as many earthly years is only a blip in time for Him. It was a gift that day. I was able to experience that understanding for a short time, but unfortunately I sometimes lose sight of it during difficult days. However, when I sit and remember how real it felt, this perspective pacifies my impatience, and I make it through another day.

In that first month, the immeasurable outpouring of love from our families, friends, neighbors, and even people we did not know, continued to astound Dan and me. Surrounded by angels from heaven and angels on earth, he and I held each other in gratitude with every act of love and service that found its way into our lives.

Neighbors and friends helped me pack up and clean our two-bedroom apartment with astounding speed and thoroughness as we prepared to move in with my dad. Dan's busy law-school friends helped transport our belongings in between rigorous studying for finals. Uplifting messages were delivered our way at the timeliest of times, as though God intended them for us to hear. None of this would have happened if good people did not follow the prophet Alma's counsel to "bear one another's burdens, that they may be light; Yea, and [be] willing to mourn with those who mourn; yea, and comfort those that stand in the need of comfort."[2] It is not a mistake that caring for each other is part of our baptismal covenant and a fundamental principle of the Church.

Moreover, it is interesting to note that Alma spoke of mourning as a direct companion to comforting. Mourning with others is hard because it requires a person to feel someone else's hurt as much as possible, and to suffer with the mourner. Sometimes we are quicker to comfort because as outsiders from the situation, we want to fix the problem and quickly soothe the pain. However, there is a period of time where pain needs simply to be validated. Upon hearing of his nephew's death, Dan's brother Jake exemplified a follower of Christ who understands this principle. Jake said one phrase over and over: "I'm sorry. I'm *so* sorry," and simply allowed Dan to cry.

The gospel provides comfort with the knowledge that we will one day enjoy the company of our loved ones who have passed on. The scale of this comfort is directly related to the magnitude of our love. In other words, knowing families are forever is only comforting because family is so important. The more you love, the more you want to continue loving. When death severs a sacred relationship, we are quick to remind the grievers to focus on the blessings of eternal families. Unfortunately, this neglects the pain that makes the promise so sweet. It is important to remember that first we mourn and then we comfort. To comfort first discounts the very reason the promise has meaning.

When we mourn with others, our minds are susceptible to the Spirit's gentle touch, encouraging us to do Heavenly Father's will. My friendship with a woman named Jamie developed because of her willingness to follow Alma's guidance. Ten days after the funeral, she approached me at the conclusion of a Relief Society meeting at church. Despite me being surrounded by many other women offering their condolences, Jamie stood there waiting until she had my attention. She appeared emotional as she tried to express her desire to take care of me, and the strong impression she'd had to do so. She offered to cook for me, do my laundry—anything at all. There was a trace of something, almost desperation, in her voice, mingled with such genuine kindness and concern. Touched by her words, I did not know how to respond, other than throwing my arms around her and embracing her, my eyes full of tears. Having only met once or twice in the few months prior, we didn't know each other, but we both felt an immediate need to change that.

That spring, we walked almost every week for two to three hours at a time, talking about everything and becoming friends. Sociable but innately shy and reserved when it comes to my personal life, I have never connected with someone outside of my family as quickly as I did with Jamie. I wanted to absorb her beautiful spirit and all the comforting words she offered my aching soul. She seemed to know what I needed to hear, even before I did. Walking through nature as the trees and leaves exploded into spring seemed a fitting way to heal and to speak of spiritual matters.

Jamie was one of many friends who sent me uplifting scriptures or quotes almost on a daily basis for a while, helping banish the hurtful thoughts that sometimes attacked and confused me. I often wonder how different my healing experience might have been if Jamie had not followed the urgent promptings she received to become my friend. She describes the persistent feeling as one she couldn't ignore—one she didn't *want* to ignore. She knew she needed to be a part of my life, but she wasn't sure why, and she didn't know how to insert herself into the life of one who had just suffered a traumatic change. Still, she tried and succeeded. While she makes fun of herself for her less-than-eloquent introduction, I recall that moment with such fondness and gratitude.

Sometimes it can be difficult to be the recipient of comfort and service. There were times when I thought I could survive this experience on my own and didn't want to bother others with my depressing grief or ask for help. Yet by allowing others to serve me, whether through physical assistance or uplifting messages, I came to understand the importance of putting pride aside. Countless blessings came into my life through the love of others. People desperately wanted to help in any way they could. Had I refused to let them in, I would have deprived them of blessings for their willingness to serve, as well as denying myself the support system I needed to survive.

Notes

1. Doctrine and Covenants 121:7.
2. Mosiah 18:8–9.

Chapter 7

Grieving Differently

A month after Ty passed away, I had a very short conversation with someone about the weather. You know how those go—it's just something to say while you walk for a few moments in the same direction. It was another cold spring day, with the threat of rain. This person and I chatted about how cold it was, and how we looked forward to the warm weather coming in a few days. I remember saying, "I can handle a couple days of bad weather as long as I get a few days of sunshine afterward."

At this point, I realized how much my mentality about Utah's fluctuating spring weather mimicked my personal grieving. It was difficult for me to be sad for extended lengths of time. The depression required so much energy that it almost seemed more taxing to give into it than to fight it. I'd make it a few hours feeling somewhat normal (and eventually could go a couple days) before I'd let myself have a deep cry. When the heaviness passed, I'd go about my day feeling peace again. My soul rained tears and then sought the sunlight. I called this repetitive process my "grief bucket." My emotions would eventually fill to the brim, so to speak, similar to those buckets at a water park that tip over and rain on screaming children who anxiously anticipate the fall. Like those children, I could feel it about to happen, and I was always afraid of the wave of feelings it would bring. But when I could not resist anymore, my grief bucket would tip and crash all over me, and then my heart would tear to pieces and physically hurt. I'd curl into a ball and make the whole world go away while I immersed myself in the pain, remembering why I didn't like to tap into those emotions. It hurt too much. But then the pain would disappear. My bucket was empty, and I felt prepared to go about my day with a sense of normalcy.

In fact, I was doing everything I could to feel normal. After three weeks with family visiting, I went back to work part-time. I joined a local rugby team. I continued trying to get my novel published. I had to stay busy. Plenty of free time only reminded me that I had too much of it because I was supposed to be caring for a baby.

Even though I stayed productive, I made time to process my emotions. On a weekly if not daily basis, I wrote on my blog. This method of journaling became a safe haven for my thoughts, my doubts, my pain and healing, and ultimately my spirituality. Writing became the most therapeutic way for me to acknowledge everything I was feeling, and it usually slowed me down long enough to let me find spiritual comfort. While I rarely called family or friends in the midst of a breakdown, within a day of writing on my blog they were able to read and respond in ways to support and uplift me. Writing allowed me to be honest with myself by sharing my feelings frequently.

It didn't take long for Dan and me to realize we grieved differently. In keeping with the stereotype for men, he did not like to talk about his emotions. As a second-year law student who just lost his only child within weeks of finals, he immersed himself in his studies. His amazing study group, who were also his best friends, studied with Dan at our house every day for hours. He focused with such intensity that there was little time or energy left to sort through his grief. The technical term would be "compartmentalization." Dan had to separate his emotions regarding Ty's death from his need to study and excel in his exams.

Nonetheless, eventually his emotions would build up and then erupt with such force that my splintered heart seemed to fracture further with his agonized cries. Hearing my husband's pain hurt more than my own because I had no control. I could not make the pain stop for him, nor could I force him to regularly talk to me about his feelings. Dan had to heal in his own time and in his own way.

Our different methods for coping became a constant hurdle between the two of us. What brought peace to one of us did not necessarily help the other. This was evident shortly after Ty's funeral. While I enjoyed watching the beautiful video and filling our walls and dressers with framed pictures, Dan commented that it was hard for him to look at the enlarged photos. He already struggled with falling asleep at night, but it was worse as of late. One night, I hesitantly suggested that he could put the pictures away if it would help him sleep. By the time I exited the bathroom, Ty's pictures lay face down on the dresser, and the framed collage that hung across from our bed now rested on the floor.

My heart fell. I hadn't really thought Dan would follow up on my feebly offered idea. How could he really not want to see the photos of Ty? I hated the sight of them lying flat and unseen against the dresser, with the blank wall staring back, only reflecting the emptiness inside me. It felt disrespectful to our little boy. But it had been my suggestion, after all. Swallowing my hurt and confusion, I slipped into bed without another word.

Sensitive and perceptive, Dan sensed my change in emotion. He confronted me on my feelings as we lay in bed, surrounded by wounded silence. With some prodding, I admitted feeling frustrated that what made me happy and gave me comfort was only a painful reminder for him. How were we going to help each other when our needs conflicted? We did not have an immediate solution that night, but we talked about how we both were feeling. Verbalizing my frustrations helped me acknowledge my feelings to a greater extent, and in turn, helped me understand Dan's point of view. We reminded ourselves of the importance of communication in any marriage, especially during difficult times. Even if we didn't know what to say or exactly how to explain what we were feeling, we needed to try. Even if we couldn't come up with an answer, it helped to know we were aware of each other's needs.

Similar situations would present themselves in the future. When Dan felt depressed, his whole countenance changed for days at a time, while my mind churned with uncertainty. Usually, Dan and I did not break down in front of each other at the same time. Inadvertently, while one of us was hurting, the other seemed to be faring well enough to offer consolation. As a result, I started to feel resentful when Dan was sad for prolonged periods of time, though I tried to hide it. At first I didn't understand my feelings, but eventually I realized I was angry at him because it reminded me that despite how busy I tried to keep myself with work and sports, I was still sad too. I didn't want to feel the weight of my grief, yet it was difficult to ignore when it was staring me in the face through the sorrowful eyes of my husband.

Our different ways of grieving were apparent time and time again along our bumpy road of recovery. However, we realized that even if it wasn't easy, it was okay as long as we talked about how we were feeling and practiced understanding one another. Neither Dan's way of grieving nor mine was wrong, and we learned to respect and honor our differences. We could see how if we didn't, this small wedge could continue to divide us until the chasm between us grew so great we could never make our away across it again. The important lesson was learning how to build a solid bridge between our differences so there would always be a way back to each other.

Chapter 8

Testimony and the Atonement

My patriarchal blessing contains one line that always put me a little on edge. The blessing encourages me to study and pray in such a way that an everlasting faith will be built to withstand any challenge that might destroy my faith or my life. When Ty passed away, it had been fourteen years since I received my patriarchal blessing at the age of thirteen. For all those years, I had wondered what trial might arise in my life that would require faith of this magnitude. Only after losing Ty did I understand the need for such fortified faith, coupled with a testimony of the gospel of Jesus Christ.

Just days before Ty's passing, I read an *Ensign* article titled "Trials and Testimony," by Paul B. Pieper. As a counselor in my ward Relief Society presidency, I had been thinking about the lesson I would teach in a few weeks and felt drawn to speak on this very topic. Now, marking exactly one month after my baby's death, I determinedly followed through with my lesson, tearful but strengthened to share my testimony on the very topic of testimonies. In his article, Elder Pieper wrote:

> *This is the moment when eternal destinies are forged in the quiet reaches of the heart and mind as we struggle to respond to a personal trial. At such moments we can choose to remember the spiritual witnesses and testimony we have received and rely on the Lord to help us through the challenge in a way consistent with His teachings and commandments. Or we can discount the sacred whisperings we have received from the Spirit and turn to our own or another's wisdom for a solution. As [the Apostle] John saw, in the end only those who choose to rely consistently and completely on their testimonies will be able to overcome all things in mortality and stand worthily before God at the last day (see Revelation 12).*[1]

A testimony cannot be a matter of convenience, called upon only in dire circumstances. A testimony needs to be built and maintained. There is a reason testimony building begins at a young age in our Primary classes and, most importantly, in the walls of our own homes. Each of us must develop through time and experience until our testimonies can be called our own. I will forever appreciate my family, my diligent youth leaders, and my life experiences, both challenging and uplifting—all of which have contributed to my testimony of this gospel. If I had not developed a testimony before losing my son, I often wonder if I would have survived.

Interestingly, a couple weeks before Ty passed away, I was asked in a routine Church interview if I had a testimony of the Atonement of Jesus Christ. As usual and without hesitation, I answered yes. I was taken off guard when my Church leader asked me to expand on my response. I had never been asked to do that before and felt silly as I nervously stumbled through my answer. I wondered what he was looking for. Was I answering correctly? While I did not have an overwhelming firsthand experience, I had seen the Atonement work in the lives of others close to me and believed it to be a true doctrine, especially as it pertained to sin and repentance. The interview continued, but I was left feeling I needed to develop a better understanding of the Atonement. This understanding did not come until about a week after Ty's funeral.

My newfound friend Jamie invited me to go walking along the Provo trail with her. We walked and talked for a couple of hours, just getting to know each other, but inevitably talking about Ty. I admitted to her that sometimes I was not sure how I was doing so well. I was even feeling a little guilty for not grieving so openly or as often as others, and thought that perhaps I was suppressing my feelings as a coping method. What else could explain the calm I felt?

That evening, Jamie left a note on my door with some thoughts she felt she really needed to share with me. In her letter she wrote:

> *Never doubt where that peace comes from. Heavenly Father knows our struggles. If you cast your burdens on the Lord, He will make you whole. I have a strong testimony of the Lord's willingness to aid us in our troubles. The Atonement applies to these situations too. Remember, Christ felt every sorrow and experienced every pain so that He would know how to help us.*
>
> *"And it came to pass that the voice of the Lord came to them in their afflictions, saying: Lift up your heads and be of good comfort, for I know of the covenant which ye have made unto me; and I will covenant with my people and deliver them out of bondage. And I will also ease the burdens which are put upon your shoulders, that even you cannot feel them upon your backs, even while you are in bondage, and this will I do that ye may stand as witnesses for me hereafter, and that ye may know of a surety that I, the Lord God, do visit my people in their afflictions."* [1]

After reading Jamie's note, I felt a surge of peace that helped me put my doubts aside. What Dan had told me early on about unseen sources sustaining us was still true; Jamie just helped put another name to it, to remind me why my peace was possible. The Atonement of Jesus Christ was working through us.

In the past when I had thought of the Atonement, my limited understanding usually directed me to the concept of sin and repentance, and how Christ can heal our self-inflicted wounds and make us whole again. However, what I have experienced through my grief is Christ's ability to heal our emotional wounds as well. While I have been taught this principle before, the feeling never hit me personally until I was engulfed in my own pain and unable to emotionally stand without help. Christ offered me a crutch to lean on until my strength returned, and even then, He never seems far when I am ready to fall again in the ups and downs of grief and healing.

About three months after Ty passed, Dan and I visited my older sister Pawnee and her family. We attended church together, and during testimony meeting, there was a lapse in speakers. My nine-year-old niece whispered to me, "What now?" I told her we would just wait for someone else to get up and share his or her testimony.

"How about you?" Rachel asked, looking innocently into my eyes. I hesitated with my response, a variety of excuses filling my head, but her question lingered. "Do you really want me to?" I asked her. She nodded and said with a serious tone, "You have good reason to."

So I stood up in front of family and strangers and shared a shortened version of the testimony I have gained through my life experiences. This included my testimony of the temple and the personal revelation that awaits anyone who enters with an honest and prayerful heart; my testimony of how we can bear one another's burdens; of compassion and service and its healing power; of families—especially of families and how this gospel allows us to be together forever; the Atonement; and the importance of sharing one's testimony so others can be strengthened in their times of need.

Indeed, our testimonies are not for our benefit alone but also to uplift others. Through Jamie's testimony and her promptings to share her impressions with me, I suddenly better understood what it means to have a testimony of the Atonement of Jesus Christ. If anyone were to ask me now, "Do you have a testimony of the Atonement?" without hesitation and with all confidence I can now answer, "Yes, I do. I really do."

And when testimony meeting rolls around each month and I wonder if I should stand, I often hear Rachel's voice in my head: "How about you? You have good reason to."

Yes, I do have good reason, and I hope to always remember that.

Notes

1. Paul B. Pieper, "Trials and Testimony," *Ensign,* Mar. 2010, 32.
2. Mosiah 24:13–14.

Chapter 9

Battling Guilt

The most persistent challenge in my efforts to heal has been guilt. Despite the emergence of research and theories about sudden infant death syndrome, there is no clear explanation to soothe the hearts of grieving parents. If anything, the lack of answers stirs up more questions and doubts in parents' minds. At least this was the case for Dan and me. Despite the powerful workings of the Atonement, he and I still felt guilty. We seemed to take turns subjecting ourselves to the "what if" questions and "if only" thoughts. We didn't blame each other and we didn't blame God, but there were times when I blamed myself, and times when Dan blamed himself.

    I am not one who enjoys dabbling in the unknown. Some days, the need for answers ate away at my comfort, as it did for my husband. We seemed worse off when we uselessly (and always independently) researched about SIDS. It was as though we needed to know without a doubt that we did nothing wrong—as though somehow that knowledge would soothe our pain.

I believe the adversary often uses guilt to destroy our peace and our testimonies. When I was alone, Satan seemed to work the hardest, putting awful thoughts into my head. One day, when I was at Dan's and my old apartment packing up our bedroom, I came across Ty's newborn footprints. I was hit with the excruciating memories of finding him under his crib blanket. I tried to hold onto the peace and comfort we had received that it was God's plan to bring Ty home early, and all the things that seemed to prepare us for his departure.

Still, the cruelest thoughts entered my mind, in a seething voice dripping with loathing: "God knew you were going to fail. And that's why everything happened the way it did." Sitting there alone in our abandoned apartment, I curled into a sobbing mess on the floor. My heart broke all over again as I thought I had failed my son—that he could be here with me if I hadn't messed up. I should have removed the blanket when the thought had crossed my mind that evening. The explanation made sense to me: God, knowing all things, knew I would make a mistake with Ty. That's why the Spirit prompted us to cherish our time with him, and prompted others to act on our behalf before they even knew what their prayers were for.

It would not be the last time Satan would inject vicious lies into my head. I struggled with these thoughts off and on for years to come, and always when I was alone and vulnerable. However, the guilt would be alleviated later when I spoke with Dan or with family and friends, who could clear my head and help me step out of the dark box Satan sought to trap me in.

I found myself trying to retrain my thinking. What if it *was* my fault? What if I did accidentally play a role in my son's death? Certainly, in some situations a family member inadvertently contributes to a child's death. Even so, Heavenly Father would not want anyone to carry that self-destructive burden. The gospel is still true, and families can still be together forever. However, for that to happen, we all must forgive ourselves and allow the Atonement to heal us.

Five weeks after Ty's passing, my husband had an experience that completely destroyed Satan's guilt-inducing grip on him. One Sunday, Dan was struggling with guilt over Ty's death, so he asked the bishop for a blessing. He said the bishop took his time in offering the blessing, allowing long pauses so inspiration could come. In this blessing, Dan was told that before he came to earth, he was given an assignment, which he wholeheartedly accepted. Dan obediently consented that he would be willing to endure the death of his son at an early age, and he agreed to suffer and overcome this.

From that moment on, Dan was filled with unwavering confidence and understanding that thwarted any guilt or confusion about our son's death. Dan laments that I wasn't there to hear the blessing, because it was not merely the words alone that brought comfort, but the confirming Spirit he felt. That confirmation has strengthened Dan and prevented him from struggling with guilt as I have.

A few days before Dan requested the blessing from the bishop, my friend Lisa said she strongly felt she needed to share a message with me. At her house, I watched her pull a tattered magazine article from a stack of papers. It was Elder Richard G. Scott's talk from October 2005 general conference. Lisa read to me the following words from that address: "You were taught and prepared for the circumstances you would personally encounter in mortality. . . . Your memory of premortal life would be kept from you to assure that it would be a valid test, but there would be guidance given to show you how to live. Our Father's plan for salvation in this life with the opportunity of returning to Him would be called the gospel of Jesus Christ."[1]

While appreciative of this message and believing the doctrine it taught, I did not put much thought into these words until after Dan's blessing. Looking back on the timing, I do not think it is a coincidence that my husband and I were both reminded of this truth within days of each other. The Lord wanted us to know that everything happened as intended. Most importantly, He wanted to remind us that we were not sent ill-prepared for this tragedy—that in fact we could learn and grow from this experience because of the many tools and blessings provided to us in the principles of the gospel. I am grateful for yet another friend who followed the promptings of the Spirit to deliver a message the Lord wanted us to hear.

Guilt is one of the most difficult obstacles to overcome after the loss of a child, and to some degree it may be a lifelong struggle for me. However, thoughts of "if only" and "what if" do nothing but create instability and heartache. We cannot change the past, whether a death or other tragedy was our fault or not. We must accept that what happened cannot be undone. We must also understand that our future is still within our control and is largely determined by our attitudes and actions.

My son had been dead for two and a half years when I finally took some major steps to leave the cycling guilt behind. Until that time, I was almost obsessed with figuring out if I played a part in my son's death. If it was my fault, I wanted to understand that so I could work on forgiving myself. Sometimes I knew I had nothing to do with Ty's death, but other times I was certain it had been my fault. Back and forth, I tormented myself with this internal struggle, unable to find resolution.

Then October 2012 general conference came along. After praying for comfort and asking Heavenly Father for help in addressing my guilt, I received my answer. Elder Shayne M. Bowen of the First Quorum of the Seventy gave a talk that touched the broken hearts of mothers and fathers everywhere. He explained how his eight-month-old son had passed away after aspirating a piece of chalk. Elder Bowen described the consuming emotions—including guilt and anger—that followed. He then spoke of the change that took place in his heart that allowed him to "look forward with hope, rather than look backward with despair."[2]

As I heard Elder Bowen's words, the Holy Ghost spoke to my heart. My obsessive guilty thoughts took a back seat as I understood where my focus should be. No good would come from debating my role in Ty's death. The how and why of his passing needed no more attention. Rather, I needed to remember his funeral and the Spirit that flooded the chapel, testifying that all is well. During general conference, I was reminded that the gospel is not about knowing all things, but instead relying on those areas where our testimony is strongest, and allowing faith to carry the rest.

Notes

1. Richard G. Scott, "Truth Restored," *Ensign,* Nov. 2005, 78–79.
2. Shane M. Bowen, "Because I Live, Ye Shall Live Also," *Ensign,* Nov. 2012.

Chapter 10
Now and Later

A week before Ty passed away, I picked up a few more hours of work at a residential treatment center called Telos. I had previously agreed to substitute as the recreation therapist (RT) and run afternoon experiential and leisure groups with at-risk teenage boys for the three months during the spring.

The Friday before Ty passed away, circumstances allowed me to bring him to work with me while all thirty boys played sports outside. I was pleased by their positive responses towards Ty. Many of the boys smiled and laughed with enthusiasm, wanting to hold him and play with him. I loved sharing Ty with them and seeing a soft side of these boys who are often negatively labeled by society as tough and uncaring, among other things. I didn't realize until later that the small act of trusting them to play with my baby would leave such an impact, as well as open doors to powerful teaching moments.

Driving home from the hospital and leaving my infant son behind on that fateful day, I remember thinking, "I'm quitting everything. I'm quitting my job. I'm giving up on trying to get published, and I'm not going to that writer's conference I'm supposed to present at in a month." Nothing seemed important anymore. None of it mattered. I also knew no one would judge me or expect differently. I deserved to quit.

But the next morning, despite waking up to the sickening, surreal reality that Ty was gone, I felt differently about my decision. The hysteria that would come and go continued to be replaced with an overwhelming calm, leading me to feel like I could and *should* do everything to stay productive in my life. Quitting all of my upcoming plans was not the right thing to do. Consequently, I emailed Karl, the RT for whom I was supposed to substitute during the spring: "Karl, I know I should not be thinking about work right now. But I have to let you know I can't sit at home doing nothing. I will go crazy with restlessness having to face an empty home where I have no motherly duties to fill my time. Please don't find another RT to cover your groups . . . I will NEED something. I will need distraction and boys to love to fill the hole in my heart."

I returned to work two weeks later. It was the best decision I could have made. Four afternoons a week for the next three months, I spent two and a half hours with three different groups of teenage boys. I loved thinking of lessons I could teach them through therapeutic groups based on life experiences, reminding even myself of the necessity to think positively and work through challenges. Spending so much time thinking about how I could impact these boys offered an immediate source for healing I may not have found elsewhere. Not that I still didn't hurt for myself and my husband, and the loss of our son. Yet, I was able to step outside of myself for a couple hours each day and find a place of normalcy. I built relationships with those teenagers and felt loved and appreciated, and received support from my coworkers. I enjoyed special experiences with those boys, whom I will always remember with fondness.

One such experience occurred on my last day, when I was working with all thirty teenagers. After I told them we were going on a "secret field trip," I heard all sorts of rumors of where I was taking them—none of which was the least bit accurate. All the boys thought we were going to do something fun and exciting.

Karl accompanied me for this final experience. We blindfolded all the boys and guided them into three large vans. Then we drove in silence (as instructed) to the Provo Cemetery. We unloaded the boys at the west entrance. One by one, the boys were scattered throughout a portion of the cemetery. Before we left each of them alone, we said, "Count to sixty, then remove your blindfold. There is an envelope with your name on it. Open it and follow the instructions." Each boy's letter instructed him to remain quiet in respect for where he sat. He was to imagine he had just passed away, with an assignment to write down his eulogy. Who would remember him? What had he accomplished? Who would attend his funeral?

After twenty minutes, we gathered the boys together to talk about life, and we allowed them to share their eulogies. Then, I took the boys for a walk through the cemetery. We stopped at the grave of a high school acquaintance of mine, who was a couple years older than me and well liked by his peers. I explained to the boys that this young man had been drawn into the wrong type of crowd and made choices that continued to pull him down a dangerous path. A few years later, he died of a drug overdose, leaving behind a devastated family who loved him so much.

I asked the Telos boys to think about why I put Now and Later candies in their envelopes. Of course, they understood that the decisions they make now will impact them later, as well as everyone around them. I told the boys there were other ways for them to be "dead" to their families—that it didn't have to be a drug overdose. Running away, unresolved conflict . . . there are plenty of ways a young man can become lost to his family without physically dying. One message I hoped to leave with the Telos boys that day was the power of choice. We all have the freedom to choose our actions and our attitudes. However, we cannot choose the consequences of our decisions, and so we must make thoughtful choices.

With one more place to show them, I led the boys to a plot of grass in the Angel Garden that was still missing its headstone. On top of a small rectangle of grass sat a framed 5 x 7 picture of a baby, propped next to two pots of yellow flowers. The mood of the group immediately became somber again as they recognized the photo.

"This is my son," I said to them. Most of the boys present had met Ty. But there were some new faces who did not know the story. So I told them about losing my son to SIDS. I referenced their mothers and their families, telling them I know how much it hurts to lose a son, wanting them to think about their own actions. I repeated over and over again, "What you do affects other people."

I took a minute to talk about the police officer who came to my home the morning Ty passed away. He is a man I will always remember as one of the few positive things from that awful day. When nothing more could be done at the hospital, and after I'd finished holding my son in my arms, this officer returned. He embraced me with a strong, comforting hug, and with tears in his eyes, he told me how sorry he was. I will never forget him because he didn't treat my loss like it was no big deal, or just part of the job. It was real and personal. It was my life, and he showed compassion. In a letter to him I wrote, "People will remember how you respond to them. And I will always remember."

Since Ty died, I have often reflected on the concept of "choice." No one is fully prepared for an unexpected tragedy. If someone had asked me years ago how I might handle losing a child, I could not have fathomed the depth of pain that accompanies such a loss. Furthermore, I wouldn't have imagined I would still choose to present at a recreation therapy conference, and pitch a novel to an editor for the first time in my life, only weeks after my child's death. I wouldn't have expected to go back to work so soon. But I did, and each success flooded me with adrenaline and confidence to recharge and lighten my soul. There was purpose in the prompting I received that I should not quit. A loving Heavenly Father knew all these things would be healthy for me.

It is not until we are faced with the ultimate challenge that we realize our potential. Less than four weeks after Ty passed away, Elder Donald L. Hallstrom gave a talk in general conference about turning to the Lord. The following words from that talk brought me encouragement: "No matter the size of the issue, how we respond can reset the course of our life. . . . [G]iving up is not an option. And, without delay, turn to the Lord. Exercise all of the faith you have in Him. Let Him share your burden. Allow His grace to lighten your load. We are promised that we will 'suffer no manner of afflictions, save it were swallowed up in the joy of Christ' (Alma 31:38). Never let an earthly circumstance disable you spiritually."[1]

An important step for me was making the decision to succeed. From the very beginning, my husband and I joined together and promised we'd make it through this trial so our family could be together forever. As Dan relentlessly pushed through his second year of law-school finals, and as I fulfilled my commitments and pursued my goals, we decided failure was not an option. I believe these early decisions allowed the Lord into our lives and created a foundation that enabled us to endure. It did not mean we would not have hard days, because everyone does, and trials are an important part of mortality. However, with the merciful help of our Heavenly Father and Jesus Christ, when we fall, we can rise again.

Notes

1. Donald L. Hallstrom, "Turn to the Lord," *Ensign,* May 2010, 78–80.

Chapter 11

Spiritual Tools

After four months without Ty in my arms, my desire to become pregnant only intensified. It felt like déjà vu all over again, wondering how long it would take to become pregnant and anticipating the worst. How long would it take for my body to get back on track after nursing for four and a half months, and how many rounds of fertility medication would it take this time? What if it took over a year again to conceive? The idea of nine months of pregnancy, let alone not knowing how long it might take to get pregnant again, filled my soul with doubt and desperation. I did not feel I could survive that long without motherhood—not especially after savoring just a taste of the purest joy.

I found myself struggling with patience and faith, wondering how the two could coincide. I had faith I would have more children; I had felt that promise in the temple. However, I questioned why God would not grant my desire to become pregnant right now. What was the purpose in making me wait? Why, when I was doing everything I could to stay positive and connected to the gospel, would Heavenly Father not ease my aching soul by helping me get pregnant sooner? I suppose my desperation was making me feel entitled to that blessing immediately, and I was losing patience.

Around this time, Dan and I were reinstating our efforts to read the scriptures together every night. One evening, we continued where we left off in the Book of Mormon and read Ether 11. I was a little bored that night, and my eyes felt dry and tired from crying while wearing contact lenses. But halfway through the chapter, I thought, "It's good we're getting back in the habit of reading, so if the Lord does need to give us a message, we'll be more likely to receive it."

Still, I was soon ready to be done with our designated reading for that night. Seeing the upcoming chapter, Dan wanted to keep reading. I consented, but to be honest I was not really in the mood. We tend to take turns reading, so Dan read the first five verses and I read the next five. I believe with all my heart that the Lord intended for me to speak the following words aloud: "And now, I, Moroni, would speak somewhat concerning these things; I would show unto the world that faith is things which are hoped for and not seen; wherefore, dispute not because ye see not, for ye receive no witness until after the trial of your faith."[1] Moroni reminds us of the miracles and blessings that come when people remain faithful, even in things they cannot see—or in my case, when promises are not fulfilled immediately. While it was certainly not the first time I had read that verse, there was something powerful about speaking the words out loud that struck me on a personal level, especially on a night when I was struggling with faith. I needed to hear myself say those words, to regain the perspective on faith that my impatience was pushing aside.

Had Dan and I not read our scriptures regularly, I may have missed the opportunity for this verse to impact me in the way that it did. The experience brought me back to the basic lesson of remaining steadfast in the gospel—prayer, scriptures, and attending the temple. They are the small gateways to heaven that we must strive to keep open in order to receive the help and comfort that the Lord *wants* to give us. I view them as part of our spiritual tools. When I think of the word "tools," I often have an image of my husband's many toolboxes. Dan learned automotive and construction skills at a young age and throughout his childhood from his father, who was a hard-working general contractor. I have always been impressed by Dan's knowledge and grateful for his knack for fixing just about anything. Because he took the time to learn about tools and how to use them, we both have reaped the benefits.

In this life, we all have access to instruments that can help us. They may not help us fix a car or patch a hole in the wall; in fact, the need for repairs may not appear as obvious to the untrained eye. However, when we are emotionally hurting or in need of a spiritual tuneup, we have access to some wonderful tools.

Priesthood blessings are one way to receive direct help from the Lord. Dan and I have relied on them numerous times throughout this process, including that life-altering moment at the hospital. After collapsing to the floor when we learned Ty could not be revived, Dan and I were given blessings of comfort. One of our friends arrived shortly after the announcement of Ty's death. His name is Elias, and given how that morning's circumstances played out for him, I have no doubt he was intended to be there for us at that moment.

Elias was supposed to be at the law-school building already, studying with earplugs in his ears and with his phone on vibrate, which would have made it impossible for him to be reached at that crucial time for us. However, during the previous night, his gout had flared up. This painful inflammation of his ankle joint usually only occurs about once a year, and as he had experienced an episode less than three months prior, Elias was surprised by the attack. By morning, the pain had intensified enough that he took medication and decided to stay home.

Around this same time, my sister-in-law Carrie called her sister to tell her about Ty. Feeling prompted, Carrie's sister contacted Elias, who lived in her neighborhood. Prayerful and heartbroken, he hastily drove to the hospital. There, with his pure faith, he gave Ty a priesthood blessing that if he could be revived he would be, but if not, that Dan and I would be comforted in knowing he had returned home to his Heavenly Father as intended. After I received a blessing of comfort from my father, Elias blessed Dan. Even though we had just lost our son, our panic and hysteria took a back seat as the room filled with the Spirit, bringing us a feeling of comfort.

I do not believe it was a coincidence that Elias was one of the few people with us at the hospital that day. Months later, when I asked him about how he came to be there with us, he explained about the painful inflammation that kept him home. He said that in his urgency to reach the hospital that morning, he didn't realize until he was in the car that the pain had immediately subsided when he heard the awful news. The gout had served its purpose in influencing Elias to stay home so he could be contacted and thus serve as an instrument in the Lord's hands to bless his friends in our time of need. It is a testimony to me that Heavenly Father knows what we need and will direct people in our path to serve on His behalf.

It would not be the last time Dan would turn to Elias for a blessing in the months to come. In fact, Elias also became one of those friends who often shared inspired messages we needed to hear, illustrating once again the need for friends to be sensitive in following promptings from the Holy Ghost. I held so much trust and faith in Elias's testimony and understanding of the gospel, as well as his ability to be in tune with the Spirit, that my hope and comfort was often restored through an exchange of messages with him. Because of the person Elias chooses to be, with his sensitive spirit and genuine nature, he played a key role in offering spiritual solace to Dan and me.

In addition to priesthood blessings, there are other spiritual gifts that can assist us when we are struggling.

We are taught, "For all have not every gift given unto them; for there are many gifts, and to every man is given a gift by the Spirit of God. To some is given one, and to some is given another, that all may be profited thereby."[2] A few of these include the gift of testimony of Jesus Christ, the gift to believe, the gift of faith to heal, the gift of faith to be healed, the gift of prophecy, the gift of tongues, and the gift of the discerning of spirits.[3] There are many spiritual gifts, and we must learn more about them in order to know which ones we possess and how to best utilize them. As with my husband's tools, it doesn't matter how many spiritual gifts we have been blessed with. If we don't realize we have them or are ignorant of their use, their purpose is wasted.

Our patriarchal blessings can help us identify which spiritual gifts we possess. I have returned to my patriarchal blessing many times in the eighteen years since I received it. There are things mentioned that I still do not understand, but since March 2010, a portion of my blessing has opened before my eyes, offering a calming reassurance that all is as it should be. Based on the spiritual gifts revealed to me through my blessing, I also understand why I am able to deal with Ty's death in the way that I have.

The Lord said, "There hath no temptation taken you but such as is common to man: but God is faithful, who will not suffer you to be tempted above that which ye are able; but will with the temptation also make a way to escape, that ye may be able to bear it."[4] I believe this promise holds true for any challenges we face. Just as an escape is provided when we are tempted, we can receive relief from the pain we suffer in our trials. God does not send us unprepared. He offers us family, friendships, charity from strangers, scriptures, prayer, the Holy Ghost, and all the encompassing gifts of the Spirit to allow us to bear anything we are given. I know God loves us and would not send us to fail. Surely, He smiles when we all use our individual gifts and talents, and heed promptings from the Holy Ghost to help ourselves and one another.

Notes

1. Ether 12:6.
2. Doctrine and Covenants 46:11–12.
3. See ibid, vv. 13–24.
4. 1 Corinthians 10:13.

Chapter 12

Power in Recreation

Because I am a recreation therapist, it is a given that I believe leisure can bring healing. There is something about immersing yourself in a favorite activity that causes you to temporarily forget your problems—to take a healthy break. Recreation allows you to enjoy memorable times with friends and family by focusing on positive experiences.

Dan and I were fortunate to attend a number of trips in the months following Ty's passing. In April, my mom and I drove to Moab, Utah, with my in-laws to explore Arches National Park. In May, Dan and I went on two river trips: one down the Colorado River with the teenage boys I worked with, and another trip (only weeks later) with the law firm that hired Dan for the summer. Then, over the Fourth of July, Dan and I spent a weekend four-wheeling in Brian Head, Utah, with my in-laws. A couple weeks after that, Dan accompanied me to Zion

National Park on another trip for my job. By the end of the summer, I'd done more hiking, camping, rafting, and four-wheeling than I had in years.

Each trip presented me with such natural beauty that I was struck with the magnificence of this earth and the Creator of it all. Sitting beneath red-rock arches and on top of forest-covered mountains, and gliding along bending rivers, all reminded me that there is something so much greater than me—an eternal plan for us to return home to heaven, just like my son had. The beautiful scenery opened my eyes with greater perspective to remember our purpose in life. Even though I was facing such a difficult challenge, I was able to feel an incredible amount of peace during these trips.

The short vacation to Brian Head with the Kiefer family illustrates such a time when recreation allowed me to step outside of my struggles. I had driven separately and was the last person to arrive at a cabin full of eight adults and six kids. The next day, just before we were about to embark on the first four-wheeling trip of the day, my mood slipped.

Being around kids seemed to trigger me often that summer. It was especially hard that it was a family vacation. I tried to imagine what it would be like to have Ty with us, and I ached for it to be real. Dan, always perceptive of my emotions, sat beside me and told me in all confidence that everything would be okay once we loaded the four-wheelers. He was right. From the minute we jumped onto the ATVs and started tearing over the trails, I was laughing and smiling. Layers of dust coated our faces, and it wasn't long before I could feel tiny grains of dirt crunching between my teeth. We immersed ourselves in nature for an amazing four-hour adventure. Filthy by the end of it, yet emotionally cleansed, I decided family and recreation were the perfect remedy.

    I could see how recreation played a role in Dan's happiness, as well. He had been under an extensive amount of pressure since March. Only a couple weeks after Ty passed away, Dan was thrust into studying for and taking his finals for his second year of law school. I still do not know how he managed to do so well, and how he was able to jump into his summer clerkship. The program was eight weeks long, and Dan spent two weeks at Lewis & Roca's main office in Phoenix and the remaining weeks in Las Vegas. Everyone knew of our situation and treated us with compassion. Still, Dan knew he had to perform to a certain standard in order to receive a job offer by the end of the summer. With little sleep, he woke up and went to work every day, realizing that two years of law school had not fully prepared him for what he needed to do. Much of the time, he had to take a risk and hope his best efforts were good enough, and he had to keep up his outgoing nature. With four months of mind and body constantly on the go and under pressure, it was little surprise when he finally cracked.

    I was at a movie with Carrie (my sister-in-law) and her friends. Three-quarters of the way through, I received a phone call from Dan. Stepping outside the theater, I could barely understand his words, and then I heard his mother on the phone. She explained that Dan was having a panic attack. He hadn't wanted to call me and ruin my movie, but she knew he needed me. I grabbed my belongings and waited for Dan and his mother to pick me up so I could be with him at home to help him feel calm again. While he has experienced anxiety during stressful events, such as important exams, I had sensed his anxiety building over the months. As a man who has always fulfilled his duties to the best of his abilities, he has never been one to quit. However, I knew his panic attack was not just about trying to secure a job. More so, it was because he did not have the luxury of free time to process Ty's death like I had.

Even while I had been working part-time in the spring, my open schedule allowed me to hang out with friends, go shopping, exercise, and fill my leisure time with activities that made me happy. Dan did not have that same opportunity. His expectations and his drive to succeed by obtaining good grades and a job for our future ended up coming first—even when what he really needed to do was sit and work through his grieving. Dan had to compartmentalize in order to survive, and unfortunately, the door to his grief bulged until it burst open and demanded attention. He took medication as needed to relieve his anxiety, and this helped tremendously. A relaxing weekend outside with the four-wheelers provided further relief. By the time I arrived at the cabin, I was comforted to see Dan's playful nature emerge, as he put his stress and anxiety on the back burner for a couple of days.

Recreation was a means of recharging our internal batteries. At the cabin in Brian Head that summer, Dan felt confident my mood would be lifted once I went four-wheeling because he had experienced an almost immediate change in his own demeanor just a day earlier. The experience reinforced my belief that adequate leisure time contributes to one's physical, spiritual, and emotional health, especially when dealing with heavy emotions and the toll they bring. To anyone who is struggling with a difficult challenge, I suggest that you go and do something fun. Even if you don't feel like it now, engage in a recreational activity you have enjoyed in the past. Go with the hope that you will enjoy it again, and you will.

 I often think about the walks I took with my friend Jamie. She came to visit me in Vegas over the summer. At Mount Charleston, we walked an easy six-mile loop, reminiscent of when we first met only months ago. We appreciated the beauty around us and the fresh air, but our favorite part was coming across a sign that read:

> *Altitude Adjustments: Only the hardiest of plants survive in the harsh environment of Charleston Peak's alpine area. Extremely low winter temperatures, snowfields that may persist during the summer, and strong winds throughout the year, all contribute to an extremely short growing season that can be cut even shorter by a careless footstep.*
>
> *Many plants in higher elevations have evolved special features to help them cope with the climate.*

Jamie and I have talked before about the types of plants, including flowers, that evolve out of difficult circumstances. They grow between rocks in high elevations, with little water and with other challenging conditions. Despite the odds, the plants' persistence allows them to thrive. Jamie and I had many discussions on trials and the hardships that everyone faces in their lives. The plants that fight for survival is our favorite metaphor. I appreciate how the trail sign describes the "harsh environment" that these plants are forced to live in, but then mentions how they "evolved special features to help them cope."

As humans, we also have the ability to develop skills and use resources for our aid. But I believe one of our greatest assets is determination. The title of the trail sign which reads "Altitude Adjustment" could just as easily be read, *"Attitude* Adjustment." That is where the ability to change and grow begins. It starts with the simple decision that no matter what, we are going to survive. From there, we too are capable of adapting to our challenging situations. By discovering what helps us the most, we too can cope.

Chapter 13

Facing Anger

A couple of months after we lost Ty, someone said to me, "It will get harder before it gets better." I remember frowning to myself and thinking I didn't believe that. I felt I was progressing well, so why would it get harder? Perhaps I was in denial and simply couldn't bear to imagine things getting worse. As it turned out, she was right. After five months, my grief suddenly accelerated, and I was silently screaming for the brakes.

Up to this point, I personified my grief as two malicious entities out to get me: Sorrow and Anger. I often described them in my blog as chasing close to my heels, trying to trap me in their snares. In my mind, I was always running. Sometimes I visualized myself in a dark, damp alley. Cloaked in dark, hooded capes, Sorrow and Anger faced me, blocking my path. In fear, I would turn from them, sprinting the other direction to escape their outstretched hands. They would not have me that day.

I felt Anger's touch off and on. One day while shopping at Target, I looked around and realized no one could possibly guess I had lost a child only weeks previously. Even I could scarcely believe it. I mentally shut my eyes as I passed the shopping cart I no longer needed for holding Ty's car seat. Inside I was shrieking, the sound muffled as though I were screaming into a pillow. I did not want to let it out. I was afraid of feeling angry and decided Anger was the enemy, along with its sidekick, Sorrow.

In trying to get pregnant again, I often felt anger accompanying my despair. However, I never embraced it. I feared it because when I was upset, I did not feel peace; rather, I would question faith and hope. I often wondered how faith and hope were supposed to coincide, even though they are constant companions in the scriptures. I *hoped* I would get pregnant and had *faith* that I would someday, but it seemed the harder I hoped, the more I hurt when it didn't happen. This seemed to damage my faith.

I wasn't sure how I was supposed to feel, but I knew I could not allow myself to be angry. I often thought that if I let myself feel the burning rage of no longer being able to hold my son, as well as the time it would take before I could hold another baby, God might punish me. Perhaps feeling angry meant I lacked faith, and why would God grant my desire to be pregnant if I didn't have faith? As a result, anger was like a growing flame inside me, but I simply wouldn't acknowledge it.

And then it happened. It had been five months since Ty died, and Dan and I were still trying to conceive another child. I'd been practically holding my breath for a few days, afraid to breathe too hard or move too much. With my period a few days overdue, I had to force myself not to take a pregnancy test. Based on my detailed (and one might say obsessive) charting, I knew I needed to wait four more days. Despite voicing some fears, I knew this was it. I felt so sure and happy, as did a handful of people who were rooting for Dan and me. Each day that passed put a smile on my face.

But my body temperature, meticulously recorded every morning, started to drop—a sign that implantation had failed. Desperate, I kept telling myself that maybe the borrowed thermometer wasn't working right, or that traveling to North Carolina and the time-zone difference might be affecting my temperature, or that this must be the rumored implantation dip.

Early Sunday morning, my period started. Dan saw my expression and knew what had happened, but I refused to cry this time. I had cried too much already and was not going to address it. I lay back in bed without a word. He put his arm around me and held me, while I felt that protective numbness creeping over me. "None of this really matters," I told myself. "It's no big deal. It will happen next time."

The words "next time" haunted me. Unable to sleep, I sat alone on the couch for a while. As I thought about the detailed process of charting and timing all over again, I felt devastated. A few warm tears fell down my face, but I stubbornly reined in the rest. A few minutes before Dan and I needed to leave for church, he joined me on the couch. "Baby, you can cry. It's okay," he said to me. I frowned without looking at him. "No. I don't want to." He put his arms around me and I scowled, holding back the tears. "No."

Finally, the tears escaped. Dan held me, as he did every time, while I released my anguish for a minute. But it was time to go to church. Abruptly I stood, grabbed some tissue, and stalked out the front door. Dan followed close to my heels, and when I reached the locked car door, he pulled me close again. I hit his chest with my forearms, fighting against everything I was feeling. At last, I erupted.

"I'm so mad!" I cried loudly, desperately, *angrily.* Once I recognized the anger, the bitter words tumbled out of my mouth. I said things I shouldn't have said. I blamed God. I didn't understand the purpose behind faith and hope. They were useless and hurtful, and I hated it all. Why did I put myself through this every time? Why did I hope so much that I was pregnant when all it did was hurt so bad? I had not felt so smothered by anger in a very long time. It consumed my faith, hope, and happiness.

Fortunately, after Dan and I attended sacrament meeting, that lingering peace fell upon me again, allowing me to breathe and calm myself. Having released the heaviness of my anger, I felt so much lighter. At my bishop's advice I sought counseling. Through talking with the bishop and my therapist, and in using other resources, I tapped into my bottled emotions and finally addressed the deep-rooted pain I had not wanted to face. My skewed beliefs were unraveled, and I learned anger was not the enemy. It wasn't even the core of the problem, but a secondary emotion—a symptom of my pain. My anger needed to be dealt with, as long as I could manage to do so in a healthy manner. Feeling angry and sad was not a weakness as I had believed; it was normal and essential in the healing process.

I am reminded of a poem from an anonymous author:

Pain stayed so long I said to him today,
"I will not have you with me anymore"
And paused there startled at the look he wore.
"I who have been your friend," he said to me
"I who have been your teacher—
All that you know of understanding love, of
 sympathy and patience, I have taught you.
"Shall I go?"
He spoke the truth, this strange unwelcomed
 guest;
I watched him leave and knew that he was
 wise.
He left a heart grown tender in my breast.
He left a far, clear vision in my eyes.
I dried my tears, and lifted up a song
Even for one who'd tortured me so long.

These words illustrate how we tend to assume our painful experiences are merely hurtful and worthless. However, when we examine those difficult times under the right light, we will find goodness. While I once battled these emotions, trying to suffocate them with denial and mislabeling them as unhealthy, I learned to recognize their importance. As I felt them and then released them, I was given a better understanding of myself. Moreover, I learned that feeling anger and sadness did not in any way negate my faith or God's willingness to answer my prayers. I learned to change the way I prayed by allowing Heavenly Father into my pain instead of fearfully blocking Him out. I communicated with Him like a child seeking advice from a loving father. "Heavenly Father," I would pray, "I'm hurting today. I feel so *angry*. Please help me through this, that I may know what to do to feel better."

There was a difference between being angry *at* Heavenly Father versus praying earnestly to Him in the midst of my pain and voicing my concerns to Him. He already knew what I was feeling, but as I prayed in this manner, an immediate connection was formed that allowed me to feel His comfort more readily. As I was honest with my Heavenly Father, I started being honest with myself. This was when my healing truly began.

During the time when I was receiving therapy, Dan and I were reading our scriptures together and once more came across the topic of faith and hope. In trying to get pregnant over the past few months, I didn't know how to hope for it without hurting my faith and feeling angry when the desired results still did not come. I didn't fully understand why faith and hope were always mentioned together. My answer came one evening in August 2010.

In the Book of Mormon, Moroni shares insight on this topic through his father Mormon's words: "And what is it that ye shall hope for? Behold I say unto you that ye shall have hope through the atonement of Christ and the power of the resurrection, to be raised unto life eternal, and this because of your faith in him according to the promise."[1]

I felt stunned as I read those words. There lay the answer to the question I had been pondering for weeks, if not months. I had been hoping for the wrong thing. Rather than putting all my emotional energy and hope towards getting pregnant, I needed to put my hope in Christ and His all-encompassing promises. Mormon's advice to have hope and faith in Christ, rather than merely hoping for my own desires, broadened my perspective. Focusing on Christ would increase my faith and my peace.

President Uchtdorf declared: "In times of distress, we can hold tightly to the hope that things 'will work together for [our] good' as we follow the counsel of God's prophets. This type of hope in God, His goodness, and His power refreshes us with courage during difficult challenges and gives strength to those who feel threatened by enclosing walls of fear, doubt, and despair."[2]

With this kind of hope, I remembered that the Lord does answer prayers. I had felt His answer to my pleading that I would have more children, and I needed to have faith that He would fulfill His promise, as He had once before. Directing my hope towards Christ almost immediately softened my desperation. In combination with talking about my deep-rooted emotions, this new understanding of hope allowed peace and patience to fill my heart once again.

Notes

1. Moroni 7:41.
2. Dieter F. Uchtdorf, "The Infinite Power of Hope," *Ensign,* Nov. 2008, 21–24.

Chapter 14

Slowing Down

It has always been in my nature to move quickly. When I was a child, my great-grandma Roberts nicknamed me "Hop, Skip, and a Jump!" to describe my ever-active state. I was a young child with a vivid imagination, which allowed me to put my high energy to creative use.

In high school, it was no surprise when I joined the track team and trained to be a sprinter. I would not say it was my favorite sport or that I looked forward to the pressure. Truthfully, I dreaded the intense training and the agony of shin splints. On the other hand, there was immense satisfaction in flying through the relays and handing off that baton to a teammate. I loved how swiftly the sprinters could move from one short distance to the next. And no matter how exhausted I felt during practice, all I had to do was take one look at the distance runners and be grateful I didn't have to run as far as they did. At every track meet, I would watch them in awe. I didn't have the heart, the physical stamina, or the least bit of desire to run such lengthy races. I would much rather exert all my energy for the duration of one brief event and get it over with.

My "sprinter's mentality" seems to have followed me throughout my life. One of the most challenging experiences of motherhood for me was how much longer it took to get everything done. Running errands outside of the house seemed to take forever as I now had to lug around a baby carrier, stop for feedings and diaper changes (or worst-case scenario: a major blowout), and handle all the little details of caring for a baby. Gone were the days when I would literally jog through a store, simply because it bored me to walk the whole distance from one end to the other. At times, I made life at home more complicated, filling my schedule with to-do lists—almost as though staying at home and caring for my baby was not good enough.

Fortunately, I learned to slow down and find value in motherhood. I wrote previously about sitting in the rocking chair with Ty in my arms, feeling the strongest impression that I just needed to enjoy holding my son and live in those precious moments. Little did I know that my lessons in slowing down were far from over.

Looking back on those first couple months after Ty passed away, I can see now how badly I wanted to skip through the pain. I still believe it was healthy for me to go back to work and to find normalcy and healing while working with those teenage boys, but I was also afraid of too much downtime and where that might allow my emotions to go.

Receiving counseling was one of the most important steps in my healing. The therapist talked to me about my tendency to "get over things quickly." He reminded me that losing a child and all the related turmoil was not something I should race through.

Taking this counsel to heart and deciding to focus on my emotional healing, I stopped trying so hard to get pregnant. I put my thermometer and charting away, determined to submit myself to God's will rather than trying to force my own desperate desires to come to fruition. Imagine my utter disbelief when, shortly after making this decision, I discovered I was pregnant! It was about six months since the loss of my son, and it took a handful of pregnancy tests for me to believe I was expecting again.

Feeling like my insides were about to burst with happiness, I casually arranged a lunch date with my husband to surprise him with this news. Dan only had twenty minutes before his next class, so we sat on the grass at a park, enjoying our Chinese food and the gorgeous September weather. As we sat together, he looked longingly at a father riding a bike with his son, and commented wistfully about the little brother that joined them.

"I want one of those," Dan said. I was about to jump out of my skin! I suggested we take a break from eating and handed him one of the three fortune cookies I had filled at home with phrases of my own. Dan read the words out loud: "A priceless gift will be delivered to your home in nine months' time." Misunderstanding the fortune to be merely a coincidence, Dan frowned and said, "Oh man, that's mean!"

I almost laughed out loud. Instead, I handed him the second cookie and said, "Here, try this one."

Dan read, "Another 'second favorite' is on its way. Time of arrival: May 8, 2011." (It was an inside joke that Dan referred to Ty and any of our future children as "second favorite," since I will always be his "favorite.") Still, Dan made an incredulous noise, thinking for just a moment how unbelievable it was that Panda Express could send us home with two slap-in-the-face fortune cookies.

By this point, I couldn't help it—I started laughing and crying simultaneously, which caught Dan's attention at last. His expression transformed as realization sank in.

"Are you serious? You're pregnant!" He barrel-hugged me, crying and smiling so big. I kept holding my pregnant stomach with laughter when I was not wiping the tears away. I'll always remember the sound of our hysterical laughter and disbelief. It was the sound of pure joy and love . . . and hope.

I do not believe the amount of time it took for me to become pregnant again was a coincidence. In order to help me fully process my grief, Heavenly Father waited to grant the one wish I wanted more than anything—the one desire I hoped would heal me and bring me happiness. When I felt I could not have it, I finally paid attention to my anger, and acknowledging and dealing with that emotion allowed me to heal.

In one therapy session, I had been asked to look at why I felt so angry. As mentioned in chapter 13, anger is a "secondary emotion," usually triggered by an emotion such as hurt or fear. I broke it down as follows: I felt angry at God when I was not pregnant. I wanted to be pregnant so I could be a mom. I wanted to be a mom so badly because I missed Ty. Ultimately, my anger was a symptom of my grief. Not getting pregnant right away helped me finally address some of my anger, and subsequently led me to receive counseling. I would not be as mended as I feel today had I continued to struggle on my own. I do not believe everyone has to feel anger in order to heal, but I do believe anyone who is grieving should take a long, close look at any emotions he or she may be feeling. This is where therapy can be helpful if a person is unable to reach these conclusions independently.

It is interesting to me that conception occurred a couple weeks after my most intense therapy session where I recognized and released my harbored anger and explored my grief. Likewise, I had come to greater spiritual understanding regarding faith and hope, granting my soul respite and peace. It is my personal belief that the rebuilding of my spiritual and emotional well-being played a role in my body's ability to conceive.

I have often thought back to that day in the nursery when I rocked Ty in my arms, feeling I should simply enjoy the time with him. Back then, I learned to slow down my daily schedule and enjoy motherhood. Now, I also understand the importance of slowing down in healing. A month after all of this self-discovery, I heard what became one of my favorite general-conference talks.

President Uchtdorf spoke about airplanes and turbulence and how different pilots address the instability. He explained:

> *A student pilot may think that increasing speed is a good strategy because it will get them through the turbulence faster. But that may be the wrong thing to do. Professional pilots understand that there is an optimum turbulence penetration speed that will minimize the negative effects of turbulence. And most of the time that would mean to reduce your speed... [W]hen stress levels rise, when distress appears, when tragedy strikes, too often we attempt to keep up the same frantic pace or even accelerate, thinking somehow the more rushed our pace, the better off we will be.*[1]

There is some truth in the oft-stated phrase "Time heals all wounds," but it is not time alone that instigates healing. Certain steps need to be taken to use that time most effectively. Putting away some of our distractions or minimizing the busyness of our daily schedule is a good place to start. Looking back on my experiences, I wish I had sought therapy sooner, rather than believing I could do it all on my own, or that I *had* to do it all on my own. I did try to rely on prayer and seeking the Spirit for comfort, but what a wonderful trifecta it is to combine time, prayer, and therapy.

In my work as a recreation therapist, the term "process" is often used to describe breaking down an experience. One of my favorite therapeutic activities to facilitate is called a "task." In short, I create a challenge such as an obstacle course or any kind of problem-solving situation that requires teamwork. The scenario may require the group of participants to move from point A to point B using designated resources, as well as following rules and boundaries. Creating such scenarios that force the participants to struggle and become frustrated or perhaps even anxious is only part of the success. One of the key elements to facilitating this type of group is talking about the experience afterwards. The group is encouraged to discuss how they felt and look at why they responded the way they did, focusing on their personality traits or the life experiences that have contributed to their way of thinking. Not only are the individuals given the opportunity for personal insight, but their peers and facilitator may also point out behavioral observations the individuals may not readily recognize on their own.

Because I was required to participate in a number of these tasks while training for my profession, I can attest to the fact that it is easier to facilitate than to be a participant. An introspective look into your life is difficult because it means taking a deep look at emotions and issues you may not want to dive into. But this is why I believe in the power of therapy as a means to self-discovery. Everyone needs a little undivided attention at times. The basic requirement is to slow down enough to put aside life's distractions and take the time to focus on yourself.

My days of training for track meets are long past. In fact, I would be lying if I said I missed dripping sweat onto a rubber track that seemed as if it should melt beneath the intense Thailand sun. However, when it comes to facing challenges, I will probably always consider myself a sprinter. Besides, there are times when plowing through and accomplishing goals has its strengths and benefits. Nonetheless, now and then, I try to remember that a steady jog is also nourishing for my heart—that a little training in endurance will benefit me in the long run. And every once in a while, perhaps I will revert back to my childish ways with a simple hop, skip, and a jump, and finally take a few moments to stand perfectly still.

Notes

1. Dieter F. Uchtdorf, "Of Things That Matter Most," *Ensign,* Nov. 2010, 19–22.

Chapter 15

Tiny Miracles

While I could barely contain my happiness, fear followed me throughout my pregnancy. Persistent thoughts that I would lose this baby often interrupted my joy. Sometimes, with quiet guilt, I also wondered if there was room in my broken heart to truly love another baby as much as I loved Ty.

A couple days after what would have been his first birthday, I had an unpleasant dream that left me shaken and disturbed. In this dream, I sat in a car with my mom and my older sister Pawnee, and we were talking about her pregnancy. Pawnee looked at me and said, "What was your baby's name again? I'm sorry, I can't remember."

I frowned, racking my own brain for his name, but I couldn't remember either. Feeling anxious and embarrassed, I asked my mom, "Do you remember? I don't know why I can't remember all of a sudden." My mom shook her head, looking as confused as the rest of us. I panicked, seeing a fleeting image of my baby boy in my mind but unable to grasp it. I started yelling and crying hysterically, "What is his name? *What is his name?*" I called Dan, believing he would know—he had to. But even Dan couldn't remember. Mortified, I screamed and sobbed, throwing myself against the back seat.

When I awoke, my eyes flew open, and in relief I thought, "Ty Edward Kiefer. That is his name." For days afterward, I could not shake off that dark, awful feeling of forgetting him. I knew it would never happen in reality, least of all to the people in my dream, but somewhere inside of me, I was hesitant to move on lest Ty be forgotten.

My fear continued even after my daughter's birth. As I cradled the symbol of my hope and happiness in my arms, I struggled to ward off the fear that sought to destroy it all. Still, I cherish the beautiful, peaceful experience that surrounded Aiyana's birth on May 17, 2011. After fourteen months without holding a child of my own, my tears alternated between reminding me how much I missed Ty, and feeling so grateful and in love with my daughter. I also cried tears of exhaustion as anxiety took hold of Dan and me.

With how light and limp Aiyana felt when she slept, flashbacks from finding Ty dead in his nursery haunted me day and night. During the day, I checked on Aiyana every five minutes, truly believing against all rationale that she would die at any moment. Nighttime was the worst. As the day moved closer to sunset, my body filled with dread in anticipation of the long night ahead of me.

I would stay awake until three, four, five in the morning, too afraid to shut my eyes longer than fifteen or thirty minutes at a time, convinced I would wake to find that Aiyana had died in her sleep.

Dan and I knew the only way to conquer this type of fear would be through reliance on the Lord and the comfort of the Spirit. We prayed together, we read our scriptures, and most helpful of all, we received a priesthood blessing from our friend Elias. The Spirit felt especially strong during the blessing. If I had perfect faith, I could have believed Elias's words and feared no more. However, since I'm mortal and imperfect, it was no easy task to put fear aside.

My thoughts turned frequently to the pioneers, especially the members of the Willie and Martin Handcart companies. Around this time, I watched the movie *17 Miracles,* which depicts their arduous trek across the plains. At times, some of these Saints felt like giving up. They were starving and sick and frostbitten, and I could not help but wonder, where was God? How could He let them suffer like this when their desires to reach Zion were righteous? Nonetheless, miracles continued to happen. They were not sweeping miracles that took away the enormity of the pioneers' trials; rather, most of these miracles were small, inexplicable blessings. They found extra food, though still meager in portion, to feed their aching stomachs for one more night. Others were granted protection from wolves and snakes. On a larger scale, one child who had died in the freezing cold came back to life through her mother's faith. These miracles happened throughout the journey. They were gifts from the Lord that helped many of the pioneers get through one more day.

Sometimes when we hear the word "miracle," we imagine an event that immediately resolves a tragedy. This did not happen for the pioneers, and it does not always happen that way for us. Sometimes we wish the Lord would just take away the trial, but often it seems He offers sufficient portions of "sustenance" instead. These may appear as small helps in various forms along our own journey, perhaps so minute that if we are not looking for them, we will probably miss them.

In my own life, a miracle followed shortly after Aiyana's birth. As I mentioned, after the first few days, I felt emotionally and physically defeated. I cried in desperation, not knowing how I could be immersed in this fear day after day and on through the nights. I wondered how long it would last—five months? Perhaps the entire first year of Aiyana's life? The task loomed over me with such heaviness that I could not imagine it would go away. Yet I hoped and prayed and focused on the incredible blessing from Elias, one that took all my faith to believe in. The comfort and promise of Aiyana's safety lay inside the blessing, but I had to accept it, to make the decision to allow that priesthood power—God's power—to work in my life.

It did not happen overnight, but as promised, little by little the fear dissipated, and I felt the weight of that anxiety begin to leave after only a week. *One week!* Aiyana's birth triggered the trauma of finding my baby boy dead in his crib, as well as the fear of being childless again. In spite of that, soon after I received this priesthood blessing, each night my ability to feel safe enough to close my eyes increased, and during the day, I grew assured that I would find my daughter alive. After only one month, I felt wonderful and stronger every day, and I thanked Heavenly Father for the speedy progress both Dan and I had made. This relief from anxiety, significantly reduced day by day because of a priesthood blessing, became our miracle.

Ridding fear from our lives has been a work in progress, and remnants do emerge now and then. I have to remind myself that this kind of fear does not come from God. True, fear can be a protector when instinct tells you to run from a bad situation. It can be the Holy Ghost warning you from danger. In contrast, fear that causes doubt and guilt and destroys peace only comes from Satan. He does not deserve the power we sometimes give him to make us feel inadequate. Instead, let us give power to our Heavenly Father by placing our faith—however imperfect it may be—in Him, knowing He understands our needs and waits for us to ask for help. Through Him, the obstacle of fear can be overcome. By His merciful grace, tiny miracles can happen.

Conclusion

Taumafai

When we face a tragedy and suffer through the aftermath, we are vulnerable. Our pain is deep and our emotions run high. With our guard down, we become susceptible to attacks from the adversary. But our vulnerability can also allow us to hear God speaking to our soul.

On Dan's mission in New Zealand, he loved attending sacrament meeting because of the way the congregation sang the hymns. The Samoan members would sing as loudly as they could, while still maintaining a spirit of reverence and respect. They sang with commitment. There was no shame if a person didn't have a good voice. Singing was about the message of the hymn and *believing* in that message. Dan says it felt like a melodic prayer. As the Lord told Emma Smith, "For my soul delighteth in the song of the heart; yea, the song of the righteous is a prayer unto me, and it shall be answered with a blessing upon their heads."[1] "Taumafai" was one of the hymns Dan memorized so he could close his eyes as he sang, allowing the power of music to permeate his soul. It did not matter that he had little voice training and used to be timid singing in public. All anxiety and self-consciousness disappeared when the Samoans harmonized together to praise God and the gospel they believed to be true.

It was eight years after Dan's mission when I held my son's lifeless body in my arms at the hospital and requested Dan to sing "Taumafai." Somewhere in our five years of marriage, this song grew to represent comfort and a way to remember Jesus Christ as our Savior. Having already learned this on his mission, Dan had passed this message onto me throughout our marriage. On days when I needed to be consoled, I would cry on his shoulder, and he would sing this song to me as he held me. The song had a way of softening my pain as it did even in the hospital. It did not matter that I didn't understand all of the Samoan words. What mattered was inviting the Lord into that moment of hurt and allowing the Spirit to translate the song's message of hope and comfort.

The three verses of the song describe challenging life events we may encounter. At the end of each description is the word "taumafai." Simply stated, the word means "try." The first two verses of the song suggest that if we are faced with hardship, we must try—to put forth effort in some way, no matter how small it may be. The chorus encourages us not to weaken from difficult things, but rather to focus on what will be gained through overcoming our challenges. The third verse reminds us that even when we fall, Jesus Christ stands firm and close, and He will bring us joy. We need only try.

Together as Dan and I held our baby and sang "Taumafai," we felt a seemingly impossible peace and calm enter the room, alleviating a portion of our anguish. From that time on, "Taumafai" became our spiritual fight-song—a song we clung to in the midst of our crucible. Family members and friends adopted the idea of taumafai—that when the road gets tough, we must keep persevering, and that with a reliance on Christ and a hope for the future, we can do all things.

It is important for each person to find his or her own taumafai. It can be anything. For my husband and me, it is this song and thinking of Ty. For others, it may be a letter or an object, or a special place to go to be alone. Whatever it is, the concept of taumafai is finding something that removes the worldly blinders that distract you from the eternal perspective—something that calls upon the Spirit and reminds you of your relationship with Heavenly Father, allowing Him to speak to you.

While I did not sing "Taumafai" every time grief held me captive, I learned to rely on the Lord for comfort. It seemed that whenever I felt buried in pain and the moments of depression would not pass, the Holy Ghost delivered messages to me to console me for another day. When I fed my spirit through constant prayer and thinking of Heavenly Father, Jesus Christ, and Ty, I seemed to find exactly what I needed to hear. Sometimes I found comfort and answers through reading scriptures; often it came from friends who were in tune with the Spirit and told me exactly what I needed to hear without even knowing it; and sometimes thoughts would come to my mind in such a way that I wondered if my son was standing next to me, whispering in my ear and holding my hand.

It is easy to doubt these spiritual moments, to overanalyze in such a way that you convince yourself you imagined the comforting thought or message. Time after time, I have learned that the more I accept the Lord's answers without skepticism, the more frequently these answers to prayers come. Receiving personal revelation takes time and patience, but most importantly, it requires faith. I have learned not to insult the Lord by praying for an answer and then questioning what I feel in my heart. It takes practice to strengthen those spiritual muscles. In athletic training, muscle memory is described as the process of repeating a movement until the body remembers the task well enough to do it without deliberate effort. Likewise, receiving personal revelation becomes easier the more we listen to and act on that inspiration.

During my darkest times, when I have felt utterly alone and consumed by torturous grief, I learned that spiritual experiences are always within our reach. The key, however, is that we do reach—that we actively seek out these pieces of heaven. As the word "taumafai" indicates, we need to try. We try as much as we know how, and the Lord will help with the rest. As Nephi teaches in the Book of Mormon, "Seek, and ye shall find."[2] When I hear that scripture, I envision a treasure hunt with spiritual riches awaiting those who willingly go gather them—almost like an Easter-egg hunt where the coveted eggs are hidden just a little deeper or a little higher than the typical person might look. The Lord wants to grant us spiritual experiences because He wants us to learn, but it does require sincere desire and wholehearted effort on our part. These spiritual moments are what allowed me to survive the hard days.

When I reflect upon the ups and downs of grief and healing, I cannot help but remember a certain willow tree. A few days after Ty's funeral, Karl (the recreation therapist from Telos, where I worked) invited Dan and me to attend a memorial in Ty's honor. All of the teenage boys and the employees also attended. With his hand on the trunk of a small, potted willow tree, Karl explained that the grassy area where we stood would be landscaped into a beautiful "peace garden." Here the tree would grow and bloom until it could offer shade and a quiet place for people to go when they were feeling sad or in need of comfort. Each of us present, including some of my immediate family members, took turns shoveling dirt around the potted willow. When the pit that held the willow was filled, Karl let go of the tree trunk and said, "Look how well this tree stands on its own when it is supported."

Not only did that tree stand on its own, but it continued to grow and bloom. By the start of summer, those flimsy, scraggly branches began to sprout lime-colored leaves. I remember having a conversation with a coworker, who commented with satisfaction, "I was worried the willow wouldn't survive the cold spring." I laughed and thought to myself, "I know exactly what you mean." The willow tree did survive that chilly spring and remains today, growing taller and fuller with every year that passes. It stands as a symbol of hope and comfort, a promise of life in the spring.

The assurance of good things to come has encouraged Dan and me to walk forward from our son's death, one step at a time. As Mosiah instructs, we must "see that all these things are done in wisdom and order; for it is not requisite that a man should run faster than he has strength. And again, it is expedient that he should be diligent, that thereby he might win the prize; therefore, all things must be done in order."[3] When Dan gave the eulogy at Ty's funeral, he shared this scripture in conjunction with a letter he wrote to Ty after he passed away. In this letter, Dan wrote, "During law school I have developed a habit of giving myself prizes at the end of a difficult semester to reward myself for all my hard work. Focusing on this prize has always allowed me to work hard when the going gets tough. You are now my reward. May I live every day in a manner that makes me worthy to be with you again. May I praise God every day for the time I had with you."

Ty is our prize—our motivation for working hard in this life, so that together, Dan and I will be with him again.

Taumafai.

Notes

1. Doctrine and Covenants 25:12.
2. 3 Nephi 14:7.
3. Mosiah 4:27.

Ty and Jesus, by Jean Keaton

About the Author

Erica Kiefer was born in Southern California to an American father whose ancestors arrived from Europe during colonial times, and a Thai mother who moved to the U.S. during high school. Adding to her rich and varied heritage, Erica grew up abroad in Asia, including Taiwan, Fiji, Thailand and Indonesia. She gained a great respect for the beautiful mosaic of cultures found in various parts of the world. After graduating from International School Bangkok, she earned a degree in recreation therapy at Brigham Young University. Her career as a recreation therapist has allowed her to work with at-risk youth since 2007.

Erica made the best decision of her life by marrying her husband in 2005. She is the mother of three, one of whom awaits her in heaven. Erica loves singing, reading, writing, and satisfying her sweet-tooth with chocolate-chip cookies. Playing collegiate rugby was one of the most memorable experiences of her life thus far.

Borrowed Angel is Erica's third published book. Her novels *Lingering Echoes* and *Rumors* were published in 2013. Learn more about Erica and her books at ericakieferbooks.com.